Spirits of the Aether

Jaq D. Hawkins

Illustrations by Jeremy Scott

www.capallbann.co.uk

Spirits of the Aether

©2001 Jaq D. Hawkins

ISBN 186163 1456

ALL RIGHTS RESERVED

No part of this publication may be reproduced, stored in a retrieval system or transmitted in any form or by any means, electronic, mechanical, photocopying, scanning, recording or otherwise without the prior written permission of the author and the publisher.

Cover design by Paul Mason
Cover illustration by Marc Potts
Internal illustrations by Jeremy Scott

Published by:

Capall Bann Publishing
Auton Farm
Milverton
Somerset
TA4 1NE

Acknowledgments

Thanks are due to many people for this last volume and for the series as a whole. First, Kevin Bullimore for starting me on this path, and secondly to Jon and Julia for believing in the project and allowing me to get on with it. People too numerous to list have contributed support, bits of information and occasionally photographs, but my thanks go out to all of them. In particular I must mention Frater M, who contributed the Alchemical Goddess associations for the correspondences chapter and Lewis Cypher for reminding me of the method of using magic squares, as well as other magical gifts which have proven very effective in times of need. Thanks also go to Dead Jellyfish, Webmaster of the <http://www.chaosmagic.com> site for his contribution of Chinese metaphysical theory, as posted on the 'Magick or Science?' discussion area of his site. Also Dennis and Linda Murphy, for introducing me to Azo, and Charles Nemo for introducing me to Chaos.

Special thanks are due to Gareth Howard Payne, whose gift of a star crystal has contributed so much to the inspirations and creativity for this series, and to my love and occasional groupie Anton, whose constant encouragement and inspiration may well give me the drive to realize my dream to become a full time writer.

This one is dedicated to Anton,
My Beautiful Dark Angel of Chaos,
For touching my Spirit
With the Maelstrom of your Love.
And as always, to Wendy.

The Author

Jaq D. Hawkins began magical study as a child and has been aware of elemental spirits from a very young age, despite a primarily urban upbringing. Her writings on various aspects of magical theory are recognized in American as well as British occult magazines and are repeated on various computer networks. Her writings on the relationship of elemental spirits to the natural laws of our world are unique to this series of books. Ms. Hawkins currently lives in East Anglia with the Love of Her Life, Anton, and an ever changing cast of odd characters which she loosely describes as her family, including Lucky the cat. She can be contacted through her website at: http://jaq.chaosmagic.com

The Illustrator

Jeremy Scott is a native of North Yorkshire where he attended Harrogate College of Arts. He has sold his artwork in private galleries as well as doing commissioned work, primarily his astoundingly realistic technical drawings. More recently, he has also become known for his striking landscapes. He has diversified his talents into designing theatre sets, illustrating children's books, and has even turned his hand to specialized interior design in San Francisco. His special talent for incorporating elemental creatures into his drawings is a valuable asset to this series.

Also By The Author:

Understanding Chaos Magic
Spirits of the Earth
Spirits of the Air
Spirits of the Fire
Spirits of the Water

In Preparation:

The Chaos Monkey
Women of Power: The Woman as Magician

Table of Contents

Introduction to the Spirits of the Elements Series 1
Chapter 1 The Nature of Aether 5
Chapter 2 Types of Aetherial Spirits 13
Chapter 3 Ancestor Worship and Monuments to the Dead 31
Chapter 4 Places to Find Aetherial Spirits 43
Chapter 5 To See Aetherial Spirits 49
Chapter 6 Aetherial Spirits in Natural Magic 57
Chapter 7 Aetherial Spirits in Ritual 65
Chapter 8 Aetherial Correspondences 75
Chapter 9 Aetherial Thought-Forms 83
Chapter 10 Divination With Aetherial Spirits 93
Chapter 11 Living With Aetherial Spirits 101
Appendix 105
Bibliography 139
Index 140

Introduction to the Spirits of the Elements Series

The Spirits of the Elements Series began when a friend of mine who is a palmist told me in a reading that I was destined to write a series of books about nature spirits. At first, I tried to associate this prediction with a series of children's books which I was working on at the time, as it involves characters and events taken directly from my studies about elemental spirits. However, my friend insisted that this was not the series of which he spoke. There would be a series of books written for an adult audience which he was looking forward to reading.

At first, I wondered if the material would have been sufficiently covered by books already in print. However, this concern melted away as the chapters began to form in my mind.

I believe in fairies. Call them what you will, I believe that the spirits of natural things, and some things which would seem at first as not natural, exist whether or not we choose to believe in them. These elemental spirits are very much a part of our world which we cannot afford to ignore or dismiss if we are to understand our own magical nature, or that which draws us into the world of magic.

The four alchemical elements are Earth, Air, Fire and Water. References to these four elements are used in many forms of

Paganism and Magic. They represent the material world for Earth, inspiration for Air, determination for Fire, and emotion for Water. There is a fifth element called Aether. This represents Spirit.

In the following chapters, I will explain the associations and correspondences which humans have attached to the element for this volume, but let's not forget that this is essentially a book about nature spirits. It is their nature that I hope to express in these pages. I also hope to offer some practical information about the methods of perceiving these spirits and perhaps inviting them into the home or into ritual practices. One must remember that these entities cannot be commanded, only invited. I strongly recommend respecting their independence. It is no accident that old tales about fairies often warn of danger, or at least trickery! More about that later.

One quick note for those who wish to see fairies; visual perception is rare but not unknown. They are not physically perceived with the eye in the same way as solid objects. If one studies the medical information learned over many years about how the eye perceives line and colour, one learns that there are receptors in the eyeball called rods and cones. The rods, which are shaped as the name would suggest, perceive line and definition while the cones, which are shaped like little round cones (what a surprise) perceive colour. The combined messages are sent to the brain and we 'see' things as a whole comprising defined shape and colour.

Seeing nature spirits requires a shift in our perception because the rods in our eyes perceive nothing from them. It is the cones which can perceive nature spirits, which is why they are so often depicted as brightly coloured and fanciful little creatures. To an extent, their shape is defined by what we expect it to be. It is also because they are perceived with the cones that they become elusive when one tries to look directly at them. Cones perceive periphially. To see a fairy, one must try to catch it with the corner of one's eye. Perhaps this is at least part of the reason that so many people find it difficult to believe that they were ever there at all...

Chapter 1

The Nature of Aether

"Every man and every woman is a star"
Aleister Crowley

Aether is the element of Spirit. It encompasses the basis for all of the other elements; Earth, Air, Fire and Water, and is believed by magicians to be the fabric of existence through which magic and creation itself transmits. It is the stuff of what Aristotle called "First Matter" or the primal source, sometimes the "first element" or "primary body". This is not a reference to a numerical sequence, but to the source of All, that which must exist in order that all else may come into being. It is, in essence, the primordial chaos of creation itself. Aristotle considered this element to be pure and incorruptible, unaffected by change and decay.

In a realm of pure Spirit, the qualities of the visible elements combine and defract like coloured light which is made separately visible through a prism, but with Spirit the prism works in both directions, bringing the qualitites of any one element into the whole of Spirit as easily as it defracts the single aspect from the whole. The element of Aether represents magic and Spirit, and the mystery of how one relates to the other.

Magic performed through the element of Aether is of the spirit. It may include practices which call on forms of Spirit such as elemental, Angelic or even demonic spirits, but is very closely generated through one's own personal spiritual essence. Aetherial magic is magic of the self, of the magician, and of the magicians relationship to the world of Spirit as an interrelated whole. It is in the realm of Spirit that one may see the interrelatedness of the other elements; the physical basis of Earth, the inspirational qualities of Air, the driving force of Fire, and the mutability of the directional capacity in the emotional nature of Water which come together into a delicate balance of magic which is what we call Spirit.

Aether has been referred to as the "fabric of space/time", the substance through which magic is transferred from source to object. It is represented by many symbols from different cultures, perhaps the most apt being the lemniscate which represents eternity. Aristotle said of his own theory of eternity that the universe in its present cosmological arrangement has never been generated in the past, and would never cease to be in the future. This is an early form of time continuum theory, wherein the scientifically accepted 'big bang' theory has no place, but the ever changing matter of the universe, like energy, is not actually created or destroyed, only transmuted. Aristotle's argument for this theory is that matter is ungenerated because if it had come to be, then something must have existed before it in order to generated it, or as a substratum, for nothing comes to be from nothing, and this is matter itself. He regards the theory of Aether as a confirmation of the belief in an eternal universe. Some of his arguments put forward in this dialogue *De Philosophia* are that;

1. The universe cannot be destroyed from outside nor from inside, because there is nothing outside of it to destroy it, and there is nothing powerful enough to destroy it from the inside.

2. Whenever a composite body perishes, its parts, which have been kept together in a counternatural position, return to their natural places. The composition of the universe, however, is harmonius and natural; therefore, the universe cannot perish.

3. If the universe were created, God himself would never destroy it, not even in order to create a new universe. For the new universe would either be worse than, equal to, or better than the present universe. All three possibilities are incompatible with the idea of an unchanging divine principle.

Obviously this last argument is based in a belief of Christian theology which was the accepted religion of the time and age, yet Aristotle's theories of the eternity of motion and time in universal physics were sometimes at odds with this theology and well ahead of the times. Aristotle, even through repudiation, has contributed significantly to modern theories of physics and cosmology, and consequently to the philosophy of magic. Belief and philosophy are mutable memes which change with time, experience and new discoveries. The scientist Lavosier postulates, and even proves by the scientific method, that Aether does not exist, because like magic itself, it cannot be detected and measured by scientific methods, therefore scientists do not believe in Aether. However, magicians continue to practice magic through it as a medium, knowing that pure Spirit will never be proven by the scientists, who often prefer to prove non-existence of that which they cannot grasp and control.

Aetherial magic can be practiced any time, and any place. Although the symbols of magic may be employed in Aetherial ritual, in actual practice these things are unnecessary. That which is of Spirit is not dependent on the material. The implements are used to focus the spirit of the magician, yet a time will come for many when the things of ritual may be transcended. The magician may still use them, balancing the symbols of the collective elements, but the transcendant magician will recognise that the objects are not strictly necessary, and will be able to perform magic as needed without the physical presence of material objects.

Aetherial spells might be used for nearly anything, but are most appropriate for such things as self-transformation, spirit contact, reaching higher consciousness or searching Akashic records, and benevolent magic bestowed on another. It might also be used for malefic magic, but this is extremely dangerous as the magic of Spirit must flow through the magician's own spiritual essence and the most experienced magicians who are capable of making use of this area of magic will usually realize that there are less risky ways to go about the purposes which may inspire the possibility.

Beliefs about Aetherial spirits are many and varied. Some believe in Angels of various sorts, some believe in classical fairies. Some feel that they are watched over by their ancestors, some believe in a pantheon of gods and goddesses or a supreme spirit who rules over all. In all of these cases, there may be found examples of a belief that invoking the assistance of these spirits can be of benefit. There are some who believe that our own spirit or soul is the only real spirit, or in some version of the 'higher self' as is depicted by Aleister Crowley's concept of the Holy Guardian Angel, a sort of cosmic twin spirit.

Some believe that Spirit may be more easily found in certain places, whether it is in a church or Temple or in a mysterious place like a fairy mist. Some tales and concepts of specific spirits evolve over time, like the perception of vampiric spirits which have been effected by both legend and fiction over time. Yet the essence of such spirits has always existed, it is only the perceptions and personifications which adapt. For the practitioner of Spirit magic, even these apparently negative spiritual forces may be put to good purpose.

Like the more physical elements, Aether is self-cleansing and self-balancing. Those who seek to abuse the world of Spirit quickly find that the 'wave' will correct itself, depleting the magical resources of one who seeks to use this form of magic for base intent, or cycling the negative energy back onto its originator. Yet one who always seeks grand ideals will find that too much positive energy will also seek balance in the world of Spirit, again depleting the energy of the practitioner and reversing its effects. More than any of the physical elements, Aether demands balance. It is in this balance that one who seeks just compensation through the darker paths may find success, yet in doing so the magician walks the fine line which can so easily move its boundaries. Spirit requires peace, not the violence of revenge. It is in seeking the peace of one's own spirit that dark spirit magic may be successfully employed.

The power of Aether, or Spirit, is the ultimate force. A person who "has spirit" can overcome any disaster, survive any catastrophe. A person who "lacks spirit" can succumb to depression at the slightest difficulty or give in to circumstances without making any effort to improve conditions. In extreme cases, the person may even fall into psychosis in order to escape the responsibility of Self. This sort of psychosis is emotionally generated rather than biological. I have seen a person who suffers from biologically induced psychosis overcome its effects through strength of spirit which allows him to seek professional help, take appropriate medication and seek internal methods for overcoming the dibilitating effects of biology out of balance. I have also seen a person with the same condition reach a level of stability which brought him to a level of functioning which seemed truly impressive, and then after overconfidently giving up his medication and support systems, the balance was tipped and he began having non-sensical delusions which led to abandoning friendships and accepting the inevitability of his own eventual self-destruction. Such is the nature of

Spirit that a moment of strength or weakness can tip the balance.

It is through strength of spirit that some people succeed where others may fail, whether it is through financial success or other forms of what some people would call "luck". Similarly, the ability to work this form of magic has the potential to accomplish seemingly impossible goals. The Aether is the stuff of infinit potential, of unformed chaos, where all possibilities exist, and even the improbable may happen if the right combination of factors are employed. The magic of Spirit is infinit in its potential. Learning to focus and direct this infinite potential is the stuff of Aether, and of magic itself.

Creation and destruction take on new meaning when applied to the realm of Aether. The potential for creating or destroying on the spiritual plane is far more frightening than the physical disruptions of such catastrophes as earthquakes, severe storms, fires or tidal waves. Yet as with these physical transformations, Spirit can be transformed through tearing down the old to recreate the new. In this is the concept of the "dark night of the soul", the complete devastation of Spirit through emotional disasters which so unavoidably tends to become a feature of the magical path. It is through tearing down old concepts and beliefs in the arena of Spirit that the magician becomes able to face his or her own strengths and weaknesses, their own darker side or "shadow" as Jung termed it, and to hopefully emerge from the test spiritually stronger and more importantly, aware of nuances of their own inner nature. This is the rebirth of Aether, the awakening of one's individual spiritual nature.

Often people will seek help from spirit entities of some description through the trials of life. Some believe that these entities are somehow amplified in places of worship or through personal devotions. Such beliefs are widespread and take many forms, from the nice lady next door who goes to a Christian church, to the Aztec sacrificing to their god, to the incense I light every morning to a statue of a goddess who did me a rather big favour once. The forms of devotion vary, but the concept behind them all is basically the same. Leaving a saucer of milk out for the fairies stems from the same concept, to appease the Aetherial spirits in whatever form we believe them to take. Even the atheist is often known to 'blow on the dice for luck' or commit some other act which may reek of superstition, but is in effect a way of petitioning an undefined spiritual force for some little edge of assistance.

The spirits of the Aether, though still attributed with alchemical correspondences and associations, are a bit different from the spirits of the physical elements in that the boundaries between the physical and the spiritual are less defined. Those things which are of the physical elements are also permeated with Spirit, and therefore the spirits of any of the elements may be regarded as Aetherial spirits. Still, there are some spirits which are not of the physical elements, and we will focus on those for the purposes of this volume as the others will have been dealt with in the appropriate volumes of this series. Some will overlap unavoidably, especially in the realm of fairies. Others, while strictly regarded as being 'of Spirit', will still encompass the balance of the elemental realms as a whole. Correspondences, as I have explained in the previous volumes of the series, are human perceptions and ways of categorizing that which interrelates in the realm of Spirit. Still we assign them in our attempts to make sense of that which transcends the definitions provided by human language. In the world of Spirit, we seek to understand those things which science is unable to weigh, measure and categorize.

In learning to understand those spiritual entities which we associate with Aether or the world of Spirit itself, we seek to understand the balance of the universe, the nature of Spirit as it applies to our own human spirits and the power of the primordial chaos which gives rise to all existence and potential. The nature of magic, as it relates to the world of Spirit, is the goal we seek to understand as we learn about the fabric of space/time, the first element, which we call Aether.

Chapter 2

Types of Aetherial Spirits

"All nature spirits are not the same as fairies; nor are all fairies nature spirits"
Lewis Spence

Some forms of spirit are not attached to anything of the material world. Others have some association with something of one of the four basic elements, and yet are 'apart' from that element and still 'of Spirit'. These include some forms of ghosts and fairies. Spirits who are not attached to the material can only be classified here as spirits of the Aether.

This is an area where belief and religion will disagree from one person to the next as to the names and features of some forms of spirit, yet there are also factors which different beliefs will generally have in common regarding them. Even many people who do not believe in the world of Spirit at all will sometimes consider the possibility of ghosts or of some sort of thought-form version of them, particularly after any sort of strange phenomena occurrance.

The extreme sceptic, who will look for some form of 'rational' explanation for any form of encounter with Aetherial spirits, even to the extent of creating explanations reliant on extremes of coincidence and twists of physics far more bizarre than the possibility of believing in spirits, is unlikely to pick

up this book and so I don't propose to make any provision for such people whatsoever.

Most people will have some form of encounter with an Aetherial spirit at some time in their lives. Whether they are able to recognize and benefit from such an experience is another matter. Many stories are told of visitations from newly deceased relatives, Angelic beings, sightings of "the wee folk" or even divine guidance. These stories are often told by people who have not had such encounters before the occasion which is related. Occasionally, one also hears a different sort of story about encounters with 'dark' spirits of some description, such as black dogs or 'demonic' entities. Interestingly, I hear such stories most often from those who are in the habit of commerce with the spiritual worlds, although the tabloids will periodically thrill us with a black dog story and the occasional ghost, sometimes even an Angelic visitation between the aliens and the latest sighting of Elvis.

Magicians and witches live in a world of the spiritual. Even the most pragmatic and scientific minded magician must take spiritual essences into account, whatever their personal explanations for them might be. The artist and magician Austin Osman Spare used to encounter spirits regularly, often allowing his artwork to be guided extensively by them. Many Pagan religions and new age beliefs include some form of spirit guides. The world of Spirit is very closely entwined with the world of magic. Although not all magic users call spirits to assist in magical operations, most will 'banish' to clear away any spiritual essences which may have been attracted by the operation at the end of a spell.

Folklore is rife with stories of encounters with spiritual entities. Most of those which are not specifically associated with elemental spirits, and some of those which are mentioned in the previous volumes of this series, fall into one of several basic categories.

Fairy hill on the Isle of Man

Wendy LeFay meditating on the fairies reputed to live in Fairy Hill

Ghosts

Ghosts are the disembodied spirits of the dead. Occasionally such a spirit will visit a loved one at the moment of death, but more often those who are seen are shadow bodies of those who have passed on. Belief systems vary on this point, but many allow that several stages of death occur as the essense of a person passes to whatever afterlife awaits. The shadow bodies therefore contain very little of the consciousness of the original person, and can become the sleepwalking spirits which are periodically witnessed repeating a pattern of something which occurred shortly before death, such as Wona of the Mist in Somerset, who is seen as an old woman in Autumn and Winter on a road going over a hill at Loxey Thorne. Like many of her kind, this ghost is seen briefly and then fades into a mist.

There are many stories of human ghosts which walk in a particular location, usually repeating a route or haunting a location where their living self once dwelt. There are also non-human ghosts which may take other forms such as animals. Because of this, many other forms of spirits are often mistaken to be ghosts.

Fairies

Fairies have been spoken of in many forms throughout this series. Beliefs of fairies include many sources for them. Christian legends claim that they are spirits of mortals who have died, or Fallen Angels. The story is that when the Fallen Angels were cast out of heaven, God commanded them "You will go to take up your abodes in crevices, under the earth, in mounds, or soil, or rocks."

Fairy beliefs of course predate Christian invasions of the countries where belief in them has continued despite the changes of religious predominance, particularly in Britain and Western Europe. They live in legends of a beautiful race which marches in armies, doing battle and performing magic, dancing drinking and participating in various revelries in a land of their own where time and space are removed from that of humans. They go by many names and titles, the best known in this country being Queen Maeve and the Tuatha de Danaan.

They are sometimes equated with underworld deities, once again associating them with the spirits of the dead. They are also sometimes depicted as manikin souls, and are represented by figures such as the Jack-in-a-box which is styled after the common Kobold. Superstitions regarding them include the belief that eating or drinking of their fare will entrap a human in the Land of Faery where time runs differently and a day of revelry can result in emerging many years later, and the belief that they cannot bear the touch of iron or salt. In pre-Christian religions, it was believed that people were taken in death not by Angels, but by fairies.

Vampyres or Demonic Spirits

Vampires have an extensive history in folklore, but here I differentiate the demonic spirit form of vampyre with the alternate spelling. Spirits which fall into this category may include the Incubus and Succubus, which were explained in *Spirits of the Fire*. The dividing line between a demonic spirit and other forms of Aetherial spirits can be largely one of interpretation, as people have been trained through Christian propaganda to think of the word 'demon' in relation to evil spirits, yet alter the spelling slightly and you have daemon, an old word for a plant spirit. A vampyre spirit takes something from the human or in some way seeks to have control over another spirit. They are often thought-form spirits, conjured by their own victims. Some who are prone to certain forms of mental illness also find that they are prone to attacks from this sort of spirit. They can often lead one to believe that a psychic attack is coming from another source, perhaps from

Location in Peel Castle where Mauthe Doo was reported to have been seen.

a trusted friend, when in fact the victim's energy is being drained by his or her own unbalanced mental forces.

The demon, on the other hand, can be a helpful spirit which does the bidding of one who summons it. It can be a natural spirit which is enticed into service, or a thought-form which is often referred to as a servitor. Either form of spirit can be sent on errands by someone who is practiced in the Arts of Magic.

On the other hand, there are also reputed to be evil spirits which would bring harm to humans, and unfortunately these are often referred to by the same name of demon. Sometimes they take the forms of such creatures as black dogs. One such which was observed in Peel castle on the Isle of Man in 1666 was the 'Mauthe Doo'. Through one of the old churches in Peel castle, there was formerly a passage to the apartment belonging to the captain of the guard. An apparition in the shape of a large black spaniel with curled shaggy hair had been frequently seen in every room, but particularly in the guard chamber, where as soon as candles were lighted, it came and lay down before the fire in the presence of all the soldiers, who at length became so much accustomed to the sight of it that they lost a great part of the terror they were seized with at its first appearance. They still, however, retained a certain awe as they believed that it was an evil spirit which only waited permission to do them hurt, and for that reason forbore swearing and all profane discourse while in its company. None cared to be left alone with it, therefore, as it was the custom for one of the soldiers to lock the gates at a certain hour and carry the keys to the captain, they agreed among themselves that whomever was to carry the keys the ensuing night, another soldier should accompany him so that no man would be exposed singly to the danger. One night, a fellow being drunk, and by the strength of his liquor rendered more daring than ordinary, laughed at the simplicity of his companions, and although it was not his turn to go with the keys, volunteered to take this office upon himself to prove his courage. All the soldiers tried to dissuade him, but the more they said, the more resolute he seemed, and swore that he desired nothing more than that Mauthe Doo would follow him, as it had done the others. After having talked in a very reprobate manner for some time, he snached up the keys and went out of the guard-room. Some time after his departure, a great noise was heard, and no one had the boldness to see what had caused it. The adventurer returned, but as loud and noisy as he had been at leaving them, he was now become sober and silent. He was never heard to speak again through all the time he lived, which was three days. The Mauthe Doo was, however, never seen after in the castle, nor would anyone attempt to go through that passage, for which reason it was closed up, and another way made.

Guardians or Watchers

Guardian spirits may include such things as House Spirits, Guardian Angels, or Watchers which are called into ritual in some traditions. Their purpose, as the name suggests, is to protect in some way. While it may seem that these sorts of spirits may often be thought-forms, they are just as often likely to be natural spirits, either of a place or in some way attached to a person.

Animal totems can be included among these spirits, as a person's affinity to a totem animal will naturally attract a spirit with the qualities of that creature. While this may be most prevalent in Shamanic cultures where belief in these totems is an accepted part of the structure of the society, it can also be true for those who seek to embrace similar beliefs although they have come from a totally different background, which applies to most of us who have grown up in Western culture. The acceptance of guardian spirits in any form allows their effectiveness.

Angels

Angels, guardian or otherwise, have become reinterpreted over the past few decades and beliefs concerning them can differ greatly from one individual to another. The word 'Angel' comes from the Greek Angelos which means 'messenger', and the Christian idea of Angels comes largely from passages in the Bible which speak of divine messages being brought to humans by Angels. Some are depicted as powerful beings who help individuals or turn the tides of wars.

Angel magic relies on these beings to perform acts of service to human magicians. This is an area primarily associated with Dr. John Dee, who wrote extensively on the heirarchies of Angels and the ruling Angels of various correspondences, some of which are included in the appropriate chapter of this volume.

More recently, Angels have been associated as higher spirits in the realms of nature spirits as well as in variations of modern new age spirituality which can fall somewhere between the Christian ideals and the nature spirit associations. Angels have become big business, and continue to fascinate the human imagination. The term is also used to denote someone who provides inspiration and instruction in some form of Art, such as the Angel of Music depicted in Andrew Lloyd Webber's *Phantom of the Opera* or my Dark Angel, referred to in this volume's dedication.

Poltergeists

More often than not, a poltergeist is a thought-form spirit. They are tricky house spirits that make things fly around or disrupt electronic equipment. Sometimes they quietly move things around at night, even furniture, to be found out of place in the morning by human residents who may be upset by the nocturnal goings on.

Unlike the thought-form spirits which we intentionally create in Temple, a poltergeist is very likely to have been manifested without the conscious knowledge of its originator. Many scientists recognize that they are known to become active in households where a girl in particular is just reaching puberty. This is sufficiently well known that it was even depicted on an episode of *The Waltons* a few decades ago, an American family show which is being shown on daytime repeats in the UK at the time of this writing (not for the first time). The hormonal changes in pubescent girls can become electromagnetically active in such a way that television and radio reception in particular are effected by the physical presence of the girl. In more extreme cases, odd phenomena as described above can occur, defying all rational explanation.

This form of thought-form activity can escalate through disruptive emotions, such as anger or fear. Poltergeist activity can be triggered by the stress of moving house, leaving the source of the disruptive energy feeling as though they have been attacked by 'ghosts' in their new home when in fact they are generating the disturbance themselves unknowingly. The activity generates fear, the fear increases the emotional disturbance and the disturbance increases activity until the vicious circle becomes unbearable. Enough of this cyclic energy can cause the disruptive energy itself to form into an independent entity, much as one might intentionally do when creating a thought-form in ritual, only this entity is not constrained by any controls. It has manifested out of wild energy, and will continue to behave indeterminently, feeding on the very emotions from which it manifested in the first place.

One wonders how many 'haunted houses' are actually 'haunted' by a disembodied spirit as described under *Ghosts*, and how many are simply the hub of wild emotions turned thought-form. There are, of course, rare exceptions where an actual ghost with a sense of humour may move things around a bit to get some attention, and by definition the playful spirit is a poltergeist. However, by and large, the nastier the activity, the more likely that it is the uncontrolled thought-form gone berserk.

These spirits are actually reasonably easy to eradicate through grounding techniques, including exorcisms. The energy can dissemble as readily as it assembled itself. The effort required will depend on the accumulated strength of the entity which may have gained momentum in a similar way that a tornado can gain strength as it travels, or it may have dissipated to very little energy if it has been ignored for some time. 'Possessed' houses such as the infamous Amityville case (the original case, before the films) invariably become more active when somebody moves in and reacts to the little things which begin to happen, escalating in proportion to the response. I always recommend 'cleansing' a house of residual spirits when moving in, as this will suffice to avoid any left over poltergeist manifestations in all but the most severe cases.

Gods

As with the spirits of the four basic elements, Aetherial spirits are known by many different names in different cultures which will also attach variations of personality to them, but most or all will fall into one of the above categories. Defining spirit entities is an inexact application of semantics at the best of times, and the spirits themselves defy rigid categorization.

Although the realm of Spirit is thought of as something which is everywhere, permeating everything, the spirits of this realm are often just as territorial as an Earth spirit may be to its tree, or an Air spirit to its mountain top. The warnings of angry spirits which one encounters regarding elemental spirits are generally much more dire as the spirits become

Icon of Pan in the forest

Another interpretation of Pan in a garden

associated as 'higher' spirits, or spirits of the realm of Spirit which we call Aether. All of them, including the Angels, are capable of angry reactions. Many of them expect certain modes of behaviour from the humans with whom they may come into contact. They may demand respect, obedience or offerings in some cases, and the penalties for neglecting these things can be formidable. Those who seek to come into contact with such spirits must allow for these requirements.

This is especially true of those who are classified as 'gods and goddesses'. Many of these entities are ancient and well established in their personalities and requirements, and to seek assistance from such an entity is to enter a realm within which *they* make the rules. I recommend studying very carefully the nature of any god forms one wishes to approach, especially when asking for favours. To an extent, Spirit entities will accommodate our perceptions of them, but very old forms become established through the perceptions of many people over time, and cannot be easily adapted by any single magician. Ancient Egyptian gods, for example, are not going to change their nature to please modern adherents. It is up to the advocates of these gods to choose to work with those who will be suitable to their own temperament and requirements.

Spirits such as ghosts or fairies may appear in different forms to various people according to their perceptions and expectations of them, although some ghosts retain the image of the person they were in life. Poltergeists in particular may appear in such a way to play on one's own fears, especially one of one's own making which is of course naturally attuned to the inner psyche of its originator. Such a spirit may also play on the other senses, even causing nausea in the hapless victim/creator.

Spirits of the Aether, whether Angel, Ghost, Demon, God or Vampyre, all have associations with a world beyond physical life, that of the realm of Spirit. Even the fairies, whom we

An Egyptian goddess altar

often think of as living spirits, are known for inhabiting the realm of Faery, a realm beyond the form of life that we know. Many religions include beliefs about some form of underworld, or province of the dead. Some believe that our ancestors continue to watch over us in some way, or to benefit from the respect that we give them when we build monuments to them after death. Recognizing this, it is only fitting that the next chapter of this volume about the spirits of the Aether should examine beliefs about the realms of the dead.

Chapter 3

Ancestor Worship and Monuments to the Dead

Ancestor worship is probably the oldest form of religion known to humankind. It predates written records in many cultures, and is most observable in aboriginal and Oriental cultures. It still thrives in these cultures in many parts of the world, both in primitive forms and in organized religion.

Ancestor worship in some form is more widespread that most Westerners would realize, even among ourselves. Elements of other cultures have permeated modern society to an extent that we are aware of the beliefs of these cultures to such an extent that even two fairly recent animated Disney films, *Mulan* and *The Lion King*, are able to depict some version of ancestor worship within the context of a story line which would have meaning to British and American children without requiring a vast leap of perceivable belief structure.

While very few of us who are born into Western society are likely to actually pray to our ancestors as someone with a different cultural background might do, it is fairly common for us to visit graves of loved ones, sometimes speaking to them aloud, even though they may be long dead and our belief paradigm one which accepts that in some form, they have long since moved on into either an afterlife or reincarnation. A psychologist would explain this as a catharsis process, but to

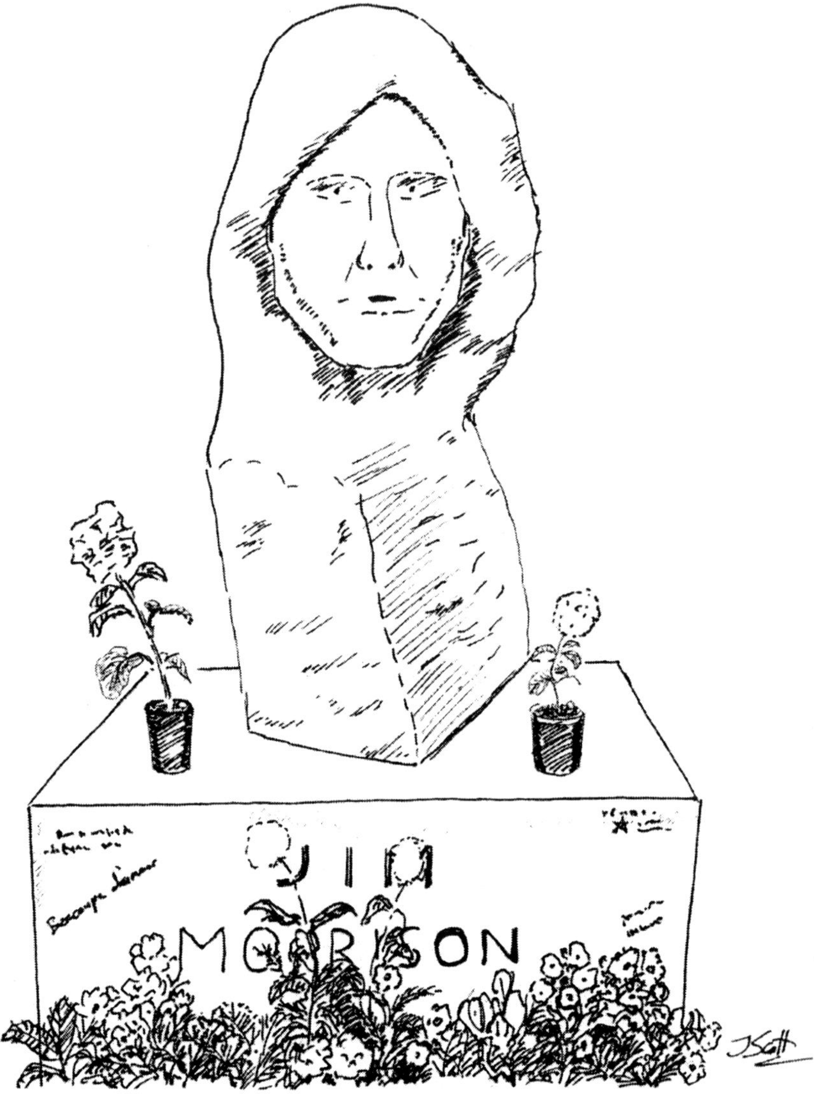
JIM
MORRISON

the person speaking to the deceased loved one, the feeling is of actually speaking to the person, with some deeply held acceptance or belief that somehow, somewhere, they are being heard by that person.

I've had little experience of this myself, but an exception occurred when I was a teenager and felt compelled to visit the grave of a grandfather I never knew. He died of a stroke four days before my first birthday, so although there may have been some sub-conscious imprint, there was no real attachment or bond between us as individuals, although my mother had told me stories of how he had favoured me over my brother when we were both babies. I was like my mother to him, and she had been his favourite child.

I knew only those things about him which my mother had told me, including some of the skeletons in his closet which we all have, yet I felt very much a part of him as I journeyed on my pilgrimage to his military grave. It was a holiday of some military significance, so it seemed appropriate to bring decorations as other people did, to show respect to a man who had been dead for fifteen years, and yet had had a part in making me the person I was becoming, despite his limited direct influence on my life.

I didn't understand the full meaning of what I was doing at the time, and was only later able to fully realize the connection. He had largely formed the person that my mother had grown to be, both genetically and influentially, and she had been the only primary adult of my childhood and had formed me in much the same way. My grandfather's dark side was apparent in the teenage discovery process I was then experiencing, as was his resourcefulness and drive. No, he had never been a serial killer or anything sinister, let's just say that his family hadn't gone short during the war.

In the minds of the living, lighting the way for the dead will help them find the next world.....or is it only to dispel the shadows?

In the catacombs of Paris, the horror of death gives way to artistic inspiration.

Memories which are passed down to us of ancestors we never knew may only serve as good stories, but sometimes they help us to understand aspects of ourselves. Although in this day and age there is more of a tendency to reject family history among many individuals and break painful connections, there seems to be something inherent in human societies to show respect for those who have come before us either through monuments or through the methods we use to dispose of their remains, traditionally through burial in the Earth with some sort of monument to mark the location, although cremation and burial at sea are also frequently practiced in Western society.

Some other cultures also dispose of remains through Fire or Water, but still the beliefs of Spirit are reflected in the ceremonies which accompany these disposal operations. Some cultures even believe that death brings divinity, and worship their own ancestors as gods as mentioned at the beginning of this chapter. What we may not realize is that their prayers to the ancestors are not so different from the tendency among Western peoples to speak to the spirits of the dead as if they were present in times of need, petitioning a dead loved one for guidance on an issue or for some relief from the grief of their physical absence. A belief in reincarnation does not preclude this tendency, we simply rationalize that the spirit of the loved one will not have moved on to the next incarnation just yet. Whether one stands at a graveside chatting away to a deceased loved one or speaks to the Aether in a belief that somewhere, the spirit is aware of the words and meanings, for at least those moments the speaker adopts a belief that they are being heard. This belief is usually strongest soon after the death of the loved one, as if the inability of the living to accept the loss of the loved one creates a belief in itself that the decomposition of the physical remains will somehow make a difference to the passing on of the spiritual essence of the person.

The Ancient Egyptians believed that preserving the body also preserved the soul of the dead, and mumified their rulers in order to preserve their divinity, believed to have been a spiritual fact in life. Alternatively, most Eastern religions which include a belief in reincarnation hold that cremation will speed the soul on to its afterlife journey toward the next life, or perhaps to release from the cycle of reincarnation to Nirvana or Godhead.

The diversity of beliefs concerning the afterlife are as varied as the cultures of the world, yet fall into a few categories; belief that death confers divinity, belief that death confers accomplishment and therefore wisdom, making the ancestor someone to consult in times of need, belief that death sends the spirit on to new realms (The Summer Land, Heaven, Nirvana, etc.), belief that death releases one to assimilate the experiences of the departed life and then to reincarnate into a new one, belief that the dead continue to walk the Earth as disembodied spirits.

Less frequently, the true Atheist will believe that death ends all consciousness and finishes the existence of the person, but this requires a belief that there is no spirit, that humans are simply material flesh and electrical impulses which extinguish after life into nothingness. Some people will even go far to dismiss stories of spiritual phenomena experienced by others in their quest to maintain this limited belief system. How sad for them, to insist so desperately on believing in nothing.

Since time immemorial and in all cultures, humans have had a fascination with the spirits of the dead. Monuments mark the resting places of the deceased in many places, and a tour through Highgate cemetery in London is all that is needed to experience much of the elaboration which different cultural influences can bring to the architecture that the living are willing, and even driven, to construct to the memories of those

The statue is long since stolen, but flowers are still left on Jim Morrison's grave in Paris

The famous lion monument in Highgate Cemetery in London, where Greek, Roman and Egyptian art forms have influenced many monuments to the dead.

Marie Laveaux's grave in New Orleans. Superstition says that if you draw three crosses on the tomb, then turn around three times, and leave an offering, the voodoo priestess will still grant your wish

whom they once knew and loved in life. Superstitions abound as to the activities of the departed spirits which are believed by many to continue to walk the Earth. Ghosts are seen all too frequently and sometimes even predictably by various observers in places of the dead and 'haunted' places. The graves of some people who were known for practicing some form of magic in life aften become places of superstition after their deaths, such as the grave of Marie Laveaux in New Orleans, where it is believed that if one makes a wish and draws three crosses on the sepulchre, as well as leaving some form of offering, the wish will manifest. Having tried this only once at that particular location, I cannot in good conscience attest that it always works. It may have been coincidence that my own wish did materialise, but then as a magician I've never really believed in coincidence.

Elaborate graves in some way can help the living feel that they have shown respect to their lost loved ones, but they also create a dramatic setting for superstition and horror films. The activities of the disembodied are not likely to be more or less prolific as a result of the decoration of the resting places of their physical remains, yet the imaginations of the living may well become more receptive to the impressions of spiritual presences in a place of the dead, and in particular to those which are embellished with creative ornamentation.

Whatever one may believe about the nature of Spirit and the dead, it is generally very easy to feel a radiance or impression of Spirit in such places. Yet regions of the dead are only one example of places where one may find Aetherial spirits.

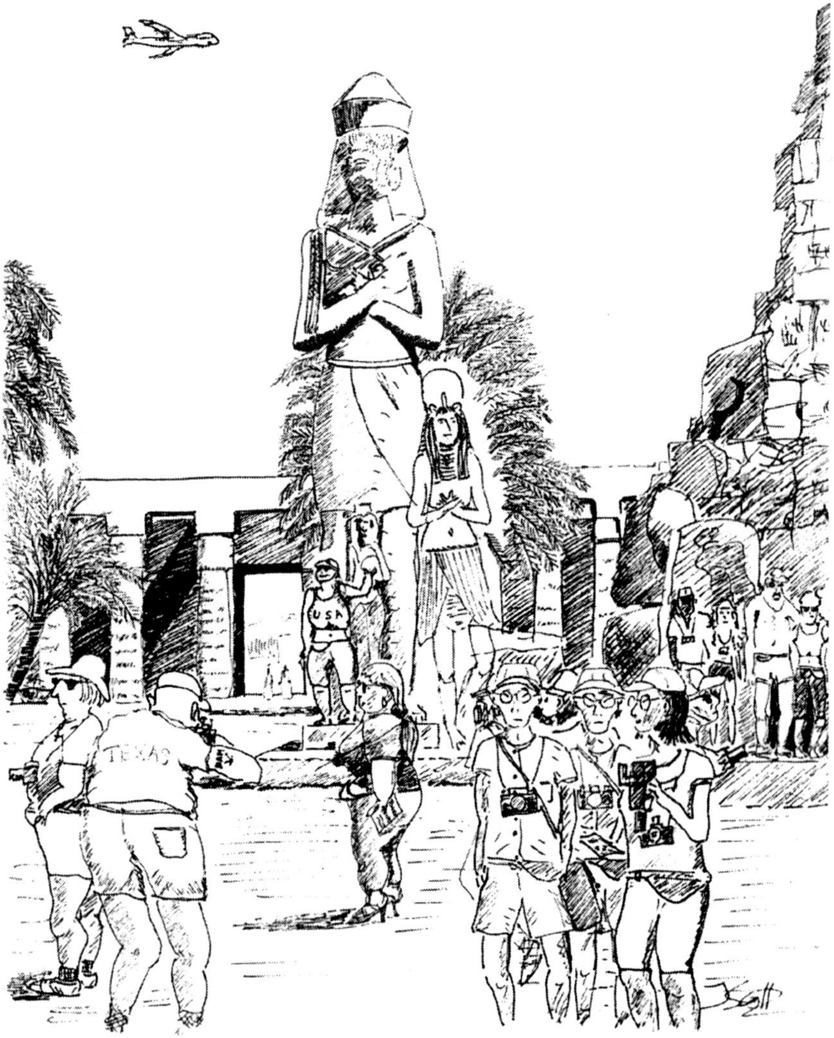
USA
TEXAS

Chapter 4

Places to Find Aetherial Spirits

"Nullus enim locus sine genio est."
For no place is without its presiding spirit
Servius

As was pointed out in the first chapter, Aetherial spirits may attach themselves to specific places even though the world of Spirit is everywhere, and the potential for attracting certain types of Spirit is unchanged by location. Angelic or vampyric spirits for example are easily attracted either intentionally or unintentionally anywhere, yet there are some places which seem to naturally attract spirit activity.

Some of these are obvious, churches and Temples or places of worship or sacrifice of any kind will retain a feeling of 'Spirit' long after the practices of homage have ceased, even many years or centuries later. Those which are in active use retain the imprint of these activities even more so. The spirits of the other elements which also inhabit a place will contribute to the overall feeling of a specific place, but such a place where stronger spirits have been intentionally and repeatedly called up will retain an impression of the Aetherial spirit, which often lies 'sleeping', just waiting to be called again.

If you were to visit an old Aztec Temple for example, the sensitive person would notice an odd duality of reactions or 'feelings'. On the one hand, the Earth amd Air spirits of the place create a calm atmosphere, where plants have overgrown and reclaimed what was once made by man. Yet those who have visited such places often describe strong and disturbing impressions of something which lies dormant, just waiting to be reawakened. The gods who were worshipped at these places were given blood sacrifices in ways that are not pretty to contemplate, and the feeling of expectation of more of the same remains.

By the same token, the benevolent spirit of a church where calm forms of worship have taken place will maintain that peaceful 'place spirit', long after the building itself has been deconsecrated by the appropriate clergy. The place spirit, like other elemental place spirits, will be a gestalt spirit which encompasses the qualities of the spirits of all of the objects and elements included in the place, but in the case of Aetherial spirits, the overall pervading feeling of the place will be dominated by this pure spirit which is often formed from the combined energies of its worshippers over time. This energy does not instantly dissipate when a ceremony of deconsecration is performed. If the building were left abandoned, it may fade over time, but if the place is reused for another purpose the calming spirit can have an effect on any new inhabitants which then 'feed' the energy back to the place spirit in a familiar form, forming a symbiotic bond of spiritual energy.

Ghosts and Watchers are naturally place spirits in many cases. Even Angelic spirits and some god forms may perform 'visitations' in connection with specific places, which then become holy places such as Lourdes, or they may frequently manifest in Temples specifically dedicated to their own specific god form. The visiting worshippers in such a place strengthen the Aetherial spirit of the place continually. The perception of the form of this sort of spirit is determined by the expectations of the worshippers.

Still, the world of Spirit continues to exist everywhere, and many people find it very relaxing to go for walks in ordinary places, like the countryside, just to enjoy the calming influence of unspoiled territory. Even those with minimal sensitivity can feel Spirit in the undeveloped places of nature. What many fail to realize though, is that civilization does not negate Spirit. The same 'calm' that some find in country walks can be found in the city, especially by those who are accustomed to urban surroundings. 'Tuning in' to Spirit can be done while walking the streets of London or Los Angeles, sitting on a bench in Amsterdam, or riding a Metro train in Paris, all of which I know from personal experience. San Francisco in particular has a strong feeling of 'Spirit' among the streets of The City, which probably began during Goldrush days but was significantly strengthened and formed through the cultural revolution of the 1960's, which has left a strong and recognizable imprint on The City even for those of us who weren't around to experience this cultural phenomenon first hand. The difference in sensing spiritual presences in city settings is that there are more distractions and more noise. There is an art to 'tuning out' the noise and distractions and experiencing Spirit which probably comes easiest to those of us who grew up in cities. It becomes like playing a radio while driving; the slight distraction actually helps consentration. Every city has it's own feel, it's own spirit.

There are more obvious Aetherial place spirits. A house which is 'haunted' for example. It may be a genuine ghost which replays some aspect of its former life which does the haunting, or just a spiritual energy which has been conjured unintentionally by previous human inhabitants of the house, if not by children or pre-teenagers performing experimental seances in an empty property. Some places like Peel Castle as described in chapter two retain malevolent place spirits.

Theories differ as to why this should occur, but once the spirit attaches to the place, it does seem to stay. One wonders what would happen if the old passage in the church of that castle were to be reopened.

As I explained in *Spirits of the Earth*, a bifurcation of energy created through the attention of humans to a place can actually create an entity which becomes a place spirit. Similarly, strong emotions such as joy or anger can contribute to intensification of these energies and determine the nature of the place spirit. A spirit of this sort begins as a disembodied thought-form which takes on a separate identity, absorbing the qualities of the local elemental spirits in the process. Some Aetherial spirits of course originate from the world of Spirit, but these are far less likely to permanently attach to a place. They are the pure Spirit forms. Spirits who attach to a place have a reason for doing so, and it usually involves some sort of human influence.

The exception to this is many places which are associated with fairies. Fairy hillsides and mounds are usually not made by mankind. These sorts of Aetherial spirits are territorial in a way that Angels, demons and others would find unnecessary. They are Aetherial spirits, and yet are Earthbound, living side by side with humans and yet in a different plane of existence, coming and going between the worlds at times.

Sometimes a place can be affected by Spirit for a time, and then revert to being an ordinary place. A fairy mist can create a change in a place temporarily making it 'of Spirit' or 'of Faery'. In the story I related in *Spirits of the Earth* and *Spirits of the Air*, the place I encountered was very much 'of Spirit' when I first encountered it, yet had become very ordinary and even changed in part of the landscape when I returned. Stories of this sort of encounter occur throughout written history, usually associated with the realm of Faery.

It is a fairly easy task to create a place 'of Spirit' for one's own use. A house Altar is one way of doing it. One need only set up a chosen icon or a selection of icons, usually from a consistent pantheon or something like a group of goddess forms, which have personal meaning to form a focal point. Additional decorations add a nice touch both aesthetically and subliminally. Think out your choices though, an Altar with Diana, Hecaté and Kali is going to attract a much different energy than one to Venus, Aphrodite and Freya. I usually prefer combining different entities from a consistent pantheon, as it becomes more balanced, although I wouldn't hesitate to combine cross-cultural representations of similar natures for a specific ritual.

Another way of creating one's own place spirit was described in *Spirits of the Earth*, where I explained the process of creating a garden spirit. The method could also be adapted for other places, either indoors or outdoors. However, I should warn that there are certain dangers to intentionally creating a spirit of a place in a place of nature, in that such a spirit is likely to quickly develop autonomy. This may be perfectly harmless, but is likely to pass out of the realm of one's own control in a very short time.

Creating a personal spirit of a place is easily done in an indoor Temple, where every element introduced into the contained space can be thought out and changed at will. All place spirits will develop some independent disposition, but such a contained place will be marked by frequent contact with one's own human spirit.

We are of course creatures of Spirit as well. If we see the human body as a Temple of Spirit, then it becomes clear that there is a direct connection between our own form of spirit and the other Aetherial spirits of various realms. It is this realization which can lead to an understanding of the nature of magic in the realm of Spirit, as we see that something as simple as a shift in perspective or intent can quickly lead to changes in the forces which move the events around us, resulting in intentional 'coincidences' and other forms of synchronicity which make things fall into place according to our own will. That is the secret behind the spirit of the magician.

Becoming aware of ourselves as 'of Spirit' can change how we see the world around us, our perspective of what is important, and can even lead to the ability to see other Aetherial entities in places of Spirit.

Chapter 5

To See Aetherial Spirits

This is an area where the spirits of the Aether stand apart from those of the basic four elements. The receptors in the eye which are described in the introduction to this series may be useful for perceiving some forms of Spirit such as fairies and may even assist in an attempt to see Angelic, demonic, or even ghostly spirits, or they may make little or no difference to perception of part of the spectrum of these spirits, as they are primarily psychically sensed. This still can result in visual perception in many instances, and yet is likely to involve the other senses just as frequently.

Various forms of these personifications of Spirit are known to manifest to ordinary people, although perhaps more often to those who are psychically sensitive (knowingly or unknowingly). Children and animals are more likely to 'see a ghost' than most adults, yet some spectres appear repeatedly to all comers in specific locations. Angelic visions and demonic manifestations are reported to reoccur to specific observers or in a chosen place, which is then dubbed as holy or haunted (even possessed) accordingly. Interestingly, these manifestations may come visually, audibly, or through a 'sense of presence' equally and yet will usually be described as an appearance.

Austin Osman Spare was often aware of spirit presences and

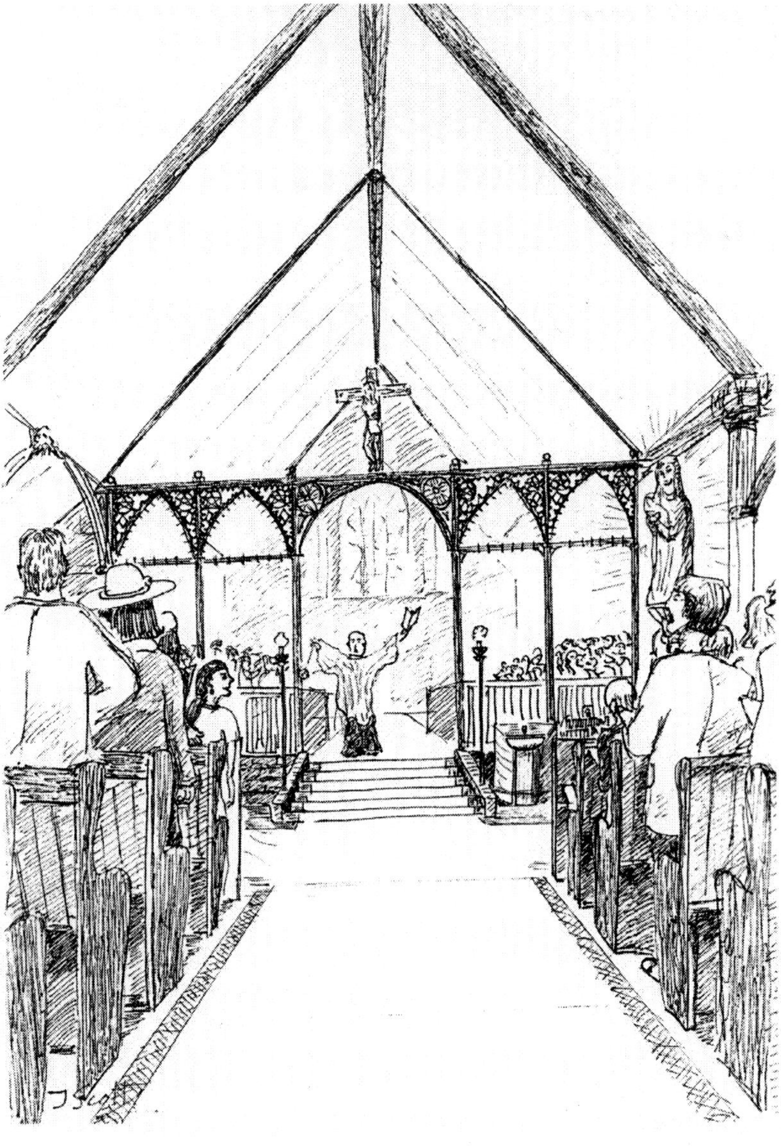

on one occasion described an experience in which he felt one walk through him, something which other, lesser known people have described periodically. Even to Spare, who was experienced in working magic with spirits and claimed that many of his drawings were channelled through them, this was a disconcerting experience.

Fleeting glimpses of Aetherial spirits may occur, but just as often a spirit may be observed strolling liesurely down a corridor for several minutes, manifesting over a holy place, or following a very frightened person for an extended period in the night. Many years ago, a person who is well-known in occult publishing described an experience to me where he was followed through a large park by a black dog. He knew through experience that it was no ordinary dog, and as the distance between them became alarmingly close, he stopped and cast a circle of protection, from where he was able to banish the dog. Despite his long experience in spirit magic, he remained in the circle until the morning light appeared to help dispel the terror.

In a case like this, one wonders if the spirit would have manifested to follow a non-occultist, or what the result would have been if perhaps a natural sensitive had attracted its attention, and yet not known how to deal with it. Does psychic ability attract spirits, or does it simply make the observer aware of what would be there anyway? It is a question that none of us is fully able to answer at present.

Those who go looking for encounters with Aetherial spirits are well advised to do their research beforehand and to be very sure of exactly what they wish to encounter, and how to deal with malevolent spirits should they attract something other than what they intend to find. While the observer may go looking for a seemingly harmless repeating ghostly manifestation or an Angelic presence which one would presume is benificent, stepping into the world of Spirit opens the senses to all manner of presences. It is generally not just because of elitism that the priestly cast of various cultures are alone allowed to communicate with Spirit, it is a matter of proper training.

To Seek Aetherial Spirits In Nature

It is not uncommon for people to seek Spirit in nature. Jim Morrison is known to have taken his 'tribe' of musicians and hangers-on out to the desert to "find God", others seek deity in forests, on the tops of hills, on the beach, near a waterfall, or any number of natural settings. If they are receptive, they will at least experience the overall spirit of the place of their choosing. This alone can be an awesome and religious experience. The difference between such a spirit and a deity form is largely one of interpretation and chosen belief. The important thing is to experience the unique elation of Spirit. Some may visually perceive a manifestation, and the possibility of this can be enhanced through ritual methods, but most who experience Spirit will be well satisfied with the sensory perception which transcends the outward senses, which become redundant by comparison. Specific rituals for seeking such an experience will be largely coloured by the belief system of the participant(s). Most often, a simple meditation with a well-contained votive candle will fit most culturally ingrained expectations. It is the participant's ability to open oneself to Spirit which is the real magic.

As with the quest to seek out elemental spirits, the chosen place should be one which is unlikely to be subject to accidental interruptions, although in this case it may be a holy place which would be populated by other seekers. Places like the Glastonbury Tor or the Chalice Well, Lourdes, certain stone circles and other recognised 'holy places' may be overrun with people of varying beliefs who seek Spirit at these sites, but they generally mind their own business and make room for others, all politely ignoring each other in their respective quests. It is not disruptive in the way that a bystander happening upon a private ritual in an out-of-the-way place might be.

Repeat visits to the same place (see *Spirits of the Earth*) are useful in that your own association of the place with the spiritual quest will help to open the psychic receptors. This is a well-known method with ghost hunters, who often repeatedly visit a place where sightings have been reported in order to observe the phenomena for themselves or to try to record it in some manner. Obviously, it would be a dangerous game to play in a place of malevolent energy. It would be interesting to try the method on one of the fairy hills of legend, such as Fairy Hill on the Isle of Man. Would a repeat visitor eventually see the host of the Tuatha De Danaan marching off on a rade? My own impressions at Fairy Hill were such that I would happily have tried this method if time on the island had permitted.

Many Spirit forms which become visible will take on an appearance which the observer expects to see. This is especially prevalent with fairies, Angels and demonic spirits. Ghosts will often resemble the previously living person, as the connection to that form maintains pattern on the astral levels for some time. Oddly, although it is most likely to be formed by the energies of at least one of its observers, a poltergeist spirit is the least likely to manifest to easy visibility. There are exceptions of course, but this sort of spirit is more likely to make its presence known through its actions. The lack of visible appearance is actually a very effective psychological artifice.

Partial visibility of one of these spirits can also be very disconcerting. In one of the well known episodes related in Kenneth Grant's *Images and Oracles of Austin Osman Spare*, Spare causes a spirit to manifest to visibility by request. As the spirit begins to take form out of a gaseous shape and something resembling two eyes appear, the observers become terrified and beg him to make it go away. Spare's own belief about this spirit is that it manifested from the subconscious of one of the observers, a classic example of a thought-form spirit. It may well have developed poltergeist activities if allowed to continue its manifestation.

Inviting a spirit into manifestation is something which should be preceded by a fair bit of forethought. Despite its literary origins, the well known version of *The Necronomicon* contains rather a lot of good advice about caution when dealing with powerful spirit entities. Old tales of various sorts advise us in how to behave when dealing with fairies, such as refusing offers of food or drink if invited into their realms, and of course we all know that one never, never invites a vampire into one's home, as this will give him access forever more.

Inviting Aetherial Spirits Indoors

Of course there are spirits which one may desire to invite into one's house or Temple. Angelic or deity spirits for example, are often invited indoors through observances at a shrine or Altar of some sort. House fairies can be invited indoors, although the type of fairy should be considered. Some can be mischievous, and the old tradition of leaving milk and honey *outside* for them is well founded.

There are always some who will become fascinated with the idea of conjuring malevolent spirits of some description into their own Temple space. Indeed, there can be legitimate reasons for the experienced magician to deal with such spirits, but of course their experience will necessarily include powerful banishing techniques for clearing their space of these spirits when they are finished with them. Dabblers in the occult can all too often get in over their heads, as teenagers in particular tend to discover periodically. All I can say to those who will dabble regardless of anyones advice otherwise is to study banishing techniques as extensively as possible from a variety of sources. You may well be grateful for the instruction at some point.

Spontaneous Sightings

As I explained in *Spirits of the Earth*, people who are stressed or enduring unusual hardship are more open to psychic impressions, and therefore prone to spontaneous spiritual sightings. Some people are naturally disposed to seeing spirits. Quite often they tend to be creative in some way; artists, musicians, poets, or people who are prone to being especially emotional, or even mad. Creative and emotional energies create a pattern of natural chaos in brain waves which are measurable by medical instruments. The chaos of emotion in the extreme can create an inner realm where words express the otherworldly disassociation with reality which accompanies the magician's domain, living on the brink of creation and destruction, which can be too much for the human mind to fully grasp.

The mind can react with depression, a common condition among many well-known artists and poets, or anxiety. Some go mad because they cannot cope with the raw power of it all. Others write the words, create the music or draw the images in their minds, which acts as a grounding mechanism and allows the pressure to escape even as it cycles back into its source, exacerbating the emotional chaos from whence it began. No wonder that so many spells are spoken in rhyme, a simple attempt to use the poetry in the soul to direct the chaos, the ultimate creative and destructive power, to an intent. The magician who holds precariously to mental balance may well be the one with the most potential magical power, if only he can direct the energy rather than allowing it to turn inwards, driving him to sure madness. Words have power to direct, and so the poet or the lyricist has direction, although the balance may always be precarious indeed. Yet the druids are known for poetic magic, and they are generally well grounded.

The ability to see spirits of any kind is something which becomes easier with practice. Some of this practice may involve ritual of some sort, which is likely to involve a form of artistic or literary expression. A ritual to conjure a spirit to visibility is likely to involve the creative use of words, as this is a method of focusing intent. Yet words are also used extensively in most forms of banishing, apart from obvious exceptions like banishing by laughter. Such 'sleight of mind' techniques are a part of what I regard as natural magic, not to be confused with the term 'Natural Magic' which well known author Marion Green has adopted for her own system of magic, but magic which comes to one naturally. One has only to observe children playing and singing rhymes to see how naturally some forms of magic, even spirit magic, come to the natural human spirit.

Chapter 6

Aetherial Spirits in Natural Magic

In natural magic, one usually thinks of directing invokations and evokations to elemental spirits of the basic four elements, with the possible exception of god and goddess forms. However, spirits of the Aether are drawn to any act of magic, and it is quite often their presence which creates the sort of 'Spirit buzz' which many people experience during acts of magic. Much of this 'buzz' comes from the magic user's own spirit, but it is often the attunement with the Aetherial spirits which instigates the elevation of spiritual awareness.

There are exceptions of course, as there are in everything. Some people have a natural affinity with their own spiritual essence and can bring on the 'buzz' from within, which in turn will again attract the attention of Spirit forms and entities. There are also individuals who have a natural affinity with some form of Aetherial spirits. I have one friend who has always dealt specifically with Angelic forms, and have known others who are naturally drawn to other specific sorts of entities in Spirit. Of course, these spirits can be intentionally invited to join in one's magic.

Dealing directly with Aetherial spirits in magic is not affected by location in the way that seeking spirits of a garden for example would be. Spirit is everywhere. However, it is often

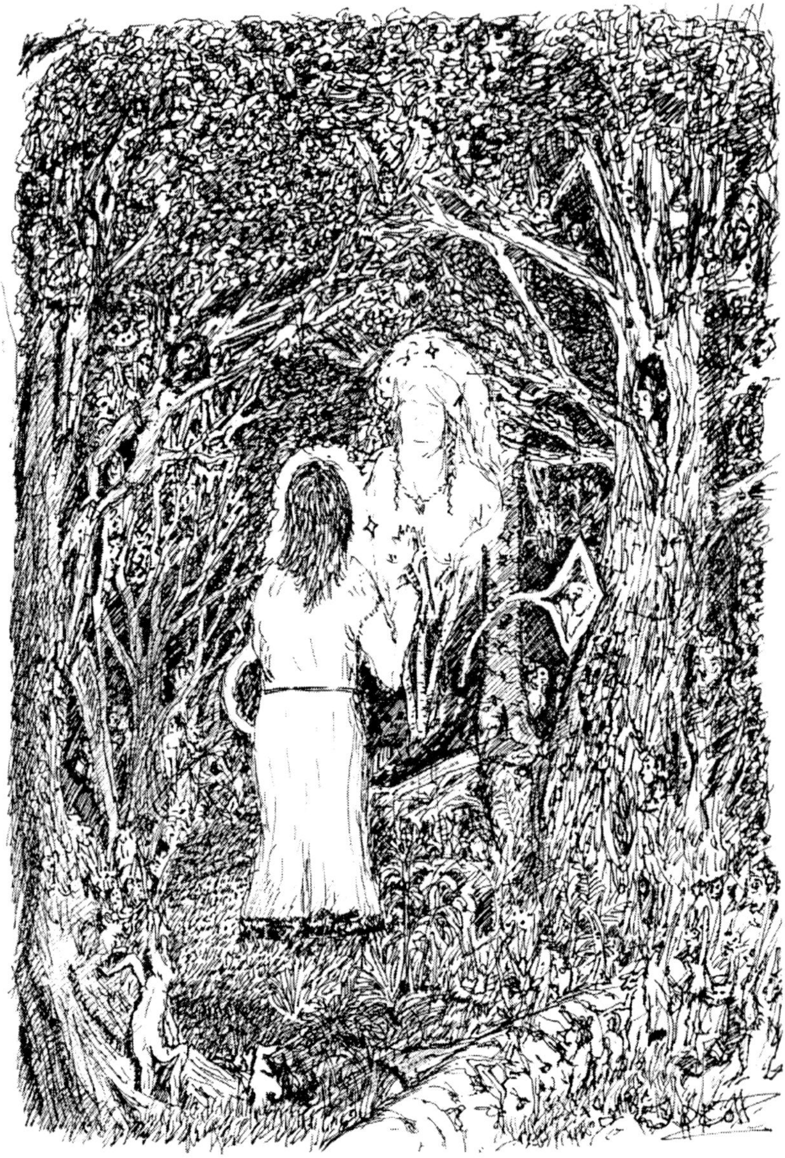

easier to tune in to Spirit in a relaxed and uninterrupted setting. The details of this can vary, and it is not essential for everyone. The experienced magician may well be able to 'tune out' the noise of the world even in a busy hospital emergency room in a pinch, but doing so takes practice and those who are just beginning to explore this area of spirit magic will find a place of quiet contemplation much more conducive to spirit contact. The imagination immediately conjures images of a quiet forest, or a meditation room with incense and candles, but a place of quiet contemplation can take many forms. In *The Magic of Findhorn*, Paul Hawken explains to us how Eileen Caddy used to sit quietly in the solitude of the public toilets to receive spirit messages. There is more to Spirit than glamour.

How to go about inviting or petitioning Aetherial spirits is a matter of individual choice. Some spirit forms can be invited through ritual, planned or spontaneous. God and goddess forms or Angelic and demonic spirits can be petitioned through some form of prayer, as is practiced in many of the world's well known religions. Aetherial spirits come easily, but whether they behave as one would wish is another matter.

The spirits of the elements are all known for independence in their own unique ways. They are not forces which can be controlled even by the most talented of magicians, but are entities which can be persuaded to be helpful if one uses the right approach. There are no guarantees. The magician who seeks to enslave a spirit entity of any sort is begging for trouble, even if s/he succeeds.

Aetherial spirits are of the realm of Spirit itself, and even less effected by human arrogance than the spirits which are attached to the things of Earth, Air, Fire and Water. They will respond very differently to someone who attempts to impose their own Will onto them than to someone who is able to share their own spiritual essence in a communion of ecstatic joining. Spirit works in a realm that feels like ecstatic love, almost sensual in its purity and yet innocent in its intent. Love unspoiled by possession.

The world of Spirit may be sought in many ways, and yet is often happened upon by accident if one is attuned to Spirit. For example, it is often in complete innocence that one accidentally happens upon Spirit in a fairy mist, something which reoccurs in many old tales and yet still happens on occasion. The legendary Land of Faery which is known to have its portals in such places as hillsides etc. is only open to those who are able to respond to Spirit.

Aetherial spirits of various sorts are often represented in a home or Temple, as god forms are represented in churches. The spirits themselves may not be contained by such representations as the world of Spirit has no physical boundaries, but the representation can form a focus or a link to the spirit form, and in some cases may even create a door between the worlds of matter and Spirit. A common form of spirit representation is a statue, plaque or even photograph of a chosen god or goddess, Angel or demonic form. Certain objects in nature are believed to attract or repel the comings and goings between the Faery realms, such as the Dobbie Stones described in *Spirits of the Water*. Some spirits and servitors may form close associations with an object representation or a piece of jewelery, allowing the magic user to directly contact this entity through the chosen object. In a recent conversation with someone very close to me, I was bewailing the difficulty of finding presents for men because many of them are not interested in the sort of cute little objects that one might buy for a woman. He told me that he uses such objects as servitors. The simple brilliance of the idea was astounding.

Using representations of spirit forms in daily magics naturally forms an affinity with the energy of the form(s). If you visit the home of someone who collects only fairy or Angel representations, the energy of that person and their home will be very different than one who has a fascination only for demonic and/or vampyre forms. Either can lead to extremes. I personally prefer to maintain a balance. My fairy collection is not all pretty representations, but includes ugly goblin-like creatures as well. My other icons span a spectrum of energies, some considered beneficient and others with worse reputations, but all of them represent an aspect of the human spirit and its attendant reality paradigms. Someone who is 'nice' all the time is as out of balance as someone who embraces negativity for its own sake. In both cases, the imbalance will be reflected in less effective magic. The natural order of magic is in balance.

Purposes which might be appropriate for involving Aetherial spirits would of course be those things which deal with Spirit itself. Self-transformation, guidance, things like the need for courage, hope or comfort, and the invokation of qualities within ourselves which need emphasizing. The forms of spells for these purposes can vary widely according to the spectrum of circumstances, but some general examples will be given in the appendix to help guide the reader to formulate specific spells for their individual needs. There are also general spells for various forms of contact with the spirit realms for its own sake, many of which fall into the category of folk magic.

Folk magic customs which relate to Aetherial spirits are most often found regarding fairies, but there are some which relate to other spirits of the Aether. It is a folk custom to weave elder twigs into a head-dress at Beltane to see spirits, and of course it is believed in many Pagan religions that Samhain is the time when the veil between the worlds is at its thinnest. Some believe that this allows one to communicate with loved ones who have passed on, while others believe that this thinning gives closer access to the Land of Faery. Again the fairy realms are associated with those of the dead.

A selection of servitors

Elder is also used to make flutes which are used to summon spirits, as well as being one of the woods used for making wands. Folk magic customs from other areas of elemental magic can be adapted to purposes of Spirit, such as the knot spell from the earlier books of this series which can be used for bringing something new into your life or a personal quality, which is magic used to effect one's own spirit.

There is certainly room for simple folk magic customs to be used along side 'higher' forms of spirit magic. These simple methods form a basis for magical technique which is proven effective in many forms, and can be adapted to 'higher' purposes, or used at face value for the more ordinary needs that all of us have from time to time, even the most talented and experienced magicians who are, after all, only human. If plaiting a few ribbons together under a rock will accomplish the purpose of making the delivery of a new washing machine show up on time, it's hardly worth the bother of performing an elaborate and complicated formal ritual to accomplish the same purpose.

Beyond the Realm of Folk Magic, the line between natural forms of magic and formal ritual magic can become thin when dealing with spirits of the Aether. John Dee is well known for Angel magic for example, which is well into the realm of ritual magic, but Angels might also play a part in daily magics for those who are attuned to them.

It can come quite naturally to some people to achieve gnosis or what Austin Osman Spare termed as 'vacuity', that state in which magic manifests. For others, ritual methods to achieve this state are necessary. Those who can learn to shift into this state at will have an advantage in magic which manifests in their daily lives. Sometimes there isn't time in a situation to perform ritual, yet the magic is urgently needed. The magician who can shift into the altered states of Spirit and perform a magical act with a simple shift of mental perspective is performing magic naturally. Yet this magic may include some commerce with extant spirits, as these spirits can be called astrally through the same mind shift which a catalyst empath might use to change the intent of a would be attacker in a very real situation. It is not so different from the shift which occurs in formal ritual, just quicker and with less external imagery.

For those who haven't yet mastered this art, there are methods for projecting an invitation to an Aetherial spirit, such as simple rhyme or poetry, even chants. They can be serious or silly, but words in metre of some form are a quick and potentially spontaneous way of calling Aetherial spirits to aid in an act of magic which is not preplanned, and of course are useful in more anticipated circumstances as well.

Wording does matter, and should be carefully chosen even in dire circumstances. Words have power, more so with Aetherial spirits, as they are the vehicle through which we project our intent. Be careful what you wish for. Variations in translation can make a big difference in results.

Aetherial spirits may be a part of one's daily life through any form of devotions or simple recognition, or simply through an awareness of their existence. One who is attuned to Spirit is likely to project an aura of calm authority and confidence. The secret to dealing with Spirit in natural magic is simply to be aware of the power of one's own spirit and its relation to the other Aetherial spirits and the realm of Spirit as a whole. Self-mastery is behind the most effective forms of magic. It is through awareness of one's own spiritual power that a basis is formed which can move into the realm of Aetherial spirits in ritual.

Chapter 7

Aetherial Spirits in Ritual

The calling of Aetherial spirits in ritual may be a very different matter from calling spirits of the basic four elements, depending on the approach of the magic user. There is a broad spectrum of practices which may fall into this chapter from petitioning god forms through prayer to the Enochian calls of John Dee which are intended to call Angelic presences. Invoking or evoking pure spirit entities from other realms are also relevant to this topic, and these might take many forms. Demonic presences conjured through the erudite rites described in *The Necronomicon* are every bit as much creatures of Spirit as the legendary denizens from the Land of Faery. An Angel, either the Christian version or the new age interpretation, is of Spirit, yet so is a Vampyre. In calling, invoking or evoking entities of Spirit, one should always keep in mind that these are very powerful essenses, not to be played with lightly.

The rituals of Magical Orders such as *The Golden Dawn* and the *Ordo Templi Orientis* are designed especially for dealing with some of these powerful spirit forms. However, joining a Magical Order is a serious business and is not easy to do, and is not an appropriate step for everyone. Still, even for those who practice solitary or primarily nature based religions, learning some of the methods of these Orders can bring useful information and I strongly recommend reading the source books which are listed in the bibliography, as some knowledge

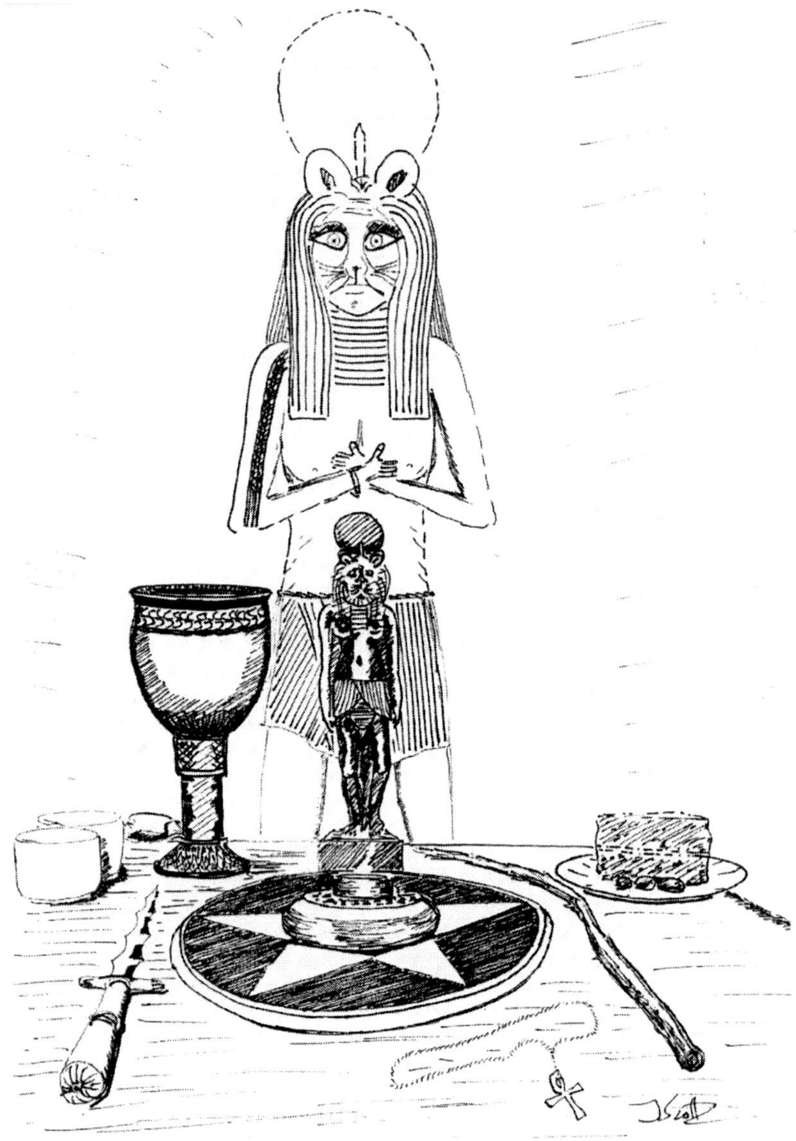

of these Orders and what they do can be useful for anyone who deals in spirit magic.

In the realm of spirits of Aether, we run into the intricacy of belief. Many who read these pages will have very definite beliefs about spirit forms and may well disagree with much that is said here. That is their perogative. As a Chaos Magician, my beliefs are very flexible and for the purposes of this chapter I will assume belief in all spirits, treating them as equally valid representations of Spirit. A Christian Angel is as valid to the person who works with that spirit form as Dora Van Gelder's Devic Angels (see *Spirits of the Earth*) are to her in her hierarchical interpretation of Faery. Individuals may interpret Spirit in different ways and symbols, but the nature of Spirit is not really effected by these variations in perspective.

The purposes for working with entities of Spirit may include a petition to a particular spirit form for some sort of assistance in everyday life, or with magical intents. An individual or group may also seek communion with Spirit as a way of bringing their own inner nature closer to that of Spirit, as at the centre of our being many of us are aware of the kinship between the human spirit and that of the divine. Self-transformation is one of the best known Alchemical concepts, and this is often approached through affinity with Spirit in some manner.

As Spirit permeates all things, the idea of bringing such spirits into the home or Temple is altered in format from that of inviting the nature spirits of the four basic elements indoors. A house spirit may be an unseen force, attracted by a belief system of the inhabitants, or it will often take the form of an icon of some sort. Most commonly statues or other depictions of a god or goddess form are used for this. Some people keep a statue of a deity on a shelf, or a painting of Jesus on a wall. The idea is similar. The physical reminder of the chosen deity promotes the affinity with that perception of deity which the person desires. There may be a difference in that most Christians will not expect their god to actually inhabit the photograph as some of the Pagan religions may believe occurs with their chosen god and goddess statues, yet either would greatly object to their representation being damaged in any way and would view an attempt to harm the picture or statue as a desecration.

House spirits may well be of other forms than deity. Many people I know have house fairies or daemons of some description, which may or may not overlap the definitions given for spirits of the other elements. I have often found that favoured statues of dragons, daemons, fairies and other things can take on personalities and even work their way into becoming house or ritual guardians, if not even helpers, as was demonstrated in the example in the previous chapter of making servitors of small statues received as gifts.

Calling Quarters

Many groups and individuals who call quarters as part of their practices will include a devotion to deity in the ceremony. It is fairly common among Wiccan groups in particular to have representations of the god and goddess on the Altar, who are addressed or called in recognition of the fifth element of Aether or Spirit, usually after the other four basic elements. This is a practice which also occurs in some forms of ritual magic.

As with the other elements, some people prefer to work with the established script of a specific magical path. Other magical practices may call Aetherial spirits of various forms according to the purpose of the ritual. Inviting a spirit into ritual is something which should be considered beforehand, and the chosen form should be carefully decided well in advance in most cases. There are exceptions of course, where a ritual in progress may require something from a spirit known to a competent magician who is taking part, but usually it is better to plan ahead. Calling powerful entities of any form, even the most benevolent, is not something to be played as a game. I personally do not call quarters in general as I see this as calling up spirits unnecessarily who have nothing to do with the ritual at hand, but others see this as an essential part of their practices. Once again, individual preferences and beliefs will vary and the world runs more smoothly if we respect the differences in each other.

Some people will call only Spirit into a ritual opening. This may de directed at a specific spirit, or generally addressed to Spirit as an entity in itself. This is something I wouldn't recommend to beginners, as leaving oneself open to undefined spirit entities is better practiced by those who know what to look for and how to react to unwanted intrusions of an undesired form.

Occasionally one may decide to create a thought-form Aetherial spirit to keep as a permanent house or Temple spirit. Again, this is for the more experienced magical practitioner as such a spirit may easily develop independence in a way that requires steady nerves and familiarity with the workings of thought-forms.

Objects which represent a specific spirit may be kept in a number of ways. They may be displayed as decoration, kept on an Altar, or put away to be brought out for ritual. This is something which must be determined by individuals according to their beliefs, space availability, and life style. A house where active children visit often and occasionally knock things over may not be good for keeping such objects openly on shelves. On the other hand, a house spirit attached to a decorative object and kept openly may influence a feeling of calm in the same house. It is very much a matter of personal choice. Less experienced magic users may wish to protect their icons by keeping them on an Altar or put away between rituals until they become proficient at instilling protection into them. In a Temple where a group habitually works, there must obviously be caretakers of such items who will see to their safety.

The attitude of the magic user who wishes to evoke a spirit form as part of an opening ritual will depend on the sort of spirit and the intent. The Wicca group calling quarters with each being done by a different person will probably expect either a Priestess or a combination of Priest and Priestess to evoke deity with an attitude of reverence. The Ceremonial Magician may evoke an Angelic presence with similar reverence, although with different methods such as John Dee's Enochian calls. Practitioners of some Faery traditions are more likely to call the Sidhe with a lighter attitude, while those who would call up favoured daemons may take a dramatic stance in order to establish parameters.

Working Outdoors

When working in the realm of Spirit, the difference in working outdoors or indoors lies only in surface things like the participants' perception of atmosphere and the privacy level. One of the arguments in the never ending debate about working skyclad is that there is hardly any use in concerning oneself whether magic can transmit through cloth if one is still wearing a house. Some people feel closer to Spirit when outdoors, especially in natural settings. Others prefer the built-up energies in their own Temple.

Icons can of course be transported to outdoor locations, but this puts them at some risk. More often, those who choose to work with Spirit in outdoor locations will do so directly, by opening themselves to Spirit psychically.

Rituals of Spirit and Food

Rituals of Spirit can take many forms. Food, which feeds both the body and the spirit, gives rise to a spectrum of ritual practices. Some of these are everyday things like rituals of food preparation which may include conscious spiritual overtones or invokations, or may simply be rituals of habit which feed a part of the spirit through repetition. Some rituals involving food are more directly conscious, such as fasting. Fasting can be a way of clearing the body as well as the mind of many of the poisons which we pour into ourselves in modern society, and is an effective practice for short periods just before major rituals as long as you don't mix it with dieting. Clearing the spirit is one thing, depriving it of sustenance is another.

Food is often present at ritual, if not as a feast then at least in the form of wine and cakes which are good for grounding the spirit after ritual. There are many spiritual traditions which involve food. Leaving treats out for the fairies is still practiced by many people today, and has been mentioned in some of the previous books of this series. Many believe that the spiritual essence of food can be taken in ritual or by fairies, and this is related to another very old practice which to my knowledge has thankfully become obsolete. This is the tradition of the Sin Eater.

In some Christian beliefs, the sins of people could be literally 'eaten' by a professional Sin Eater who would come to the home of the recently deceased and perform rituals over the body which included devouring on the spot a massive feast as well as being paid with coins. In the course of the ritual, the Sin Eater was to absorb the essence of the dead person's wrong doings of a lifetime, collecting a massive amount of negative energy which he could only hope would be 'eaten' by another Sin Eater on his death. So, think about the Sin Eater next time you complain about your present job!

Interestingly, a similar practice arises in modern magical methods where something which is to be eaten is 'charged' with a specific purpose. There are many ways of doing this, my own favourite being to draw sigils on cakes in some manner. A bit of cocoa power mixed with warm water makes a good 'ink' for drawing on marzipan, which can be included into a finished cake, and even iced over if for some reason the sigil needs concealing. Sometimes specific foods become associated with a spiritual purpose in both old and new traditions. Certain foods are known in religious rituals, especially in the Jewish religion, and many Pagans I know still have pancakes on Shrove Tuesday despite the Christian associations. Foods can become associated with ritual practices through experience, and the reader may wish to establish such rituals for their own purposes. The associations brought up by foods which are only used for specific purposes form a bond in the mind of the practitioner(s) between that specific food and the ritual purpose. For example, I know a vegetarian family who eat meat only on Samhain, using the altered perceptions caused by the drastic change in nutrition toward their celebration rituals, and I have developed a personal association between my own home made lasagna (which is very different from what you can get in a pub) to a shape-shifting ritual which feeds my spirit in ways that nothing else ever can. Ecstatic experience can take many forms.

Ritual and Spirit

Aetherial spirits, especially deity forms, are often called into celebratory rituals but might also be called in to assist acts of magic. The choice of a spirit to assist in the act of magic should be determined by the intent, and carefully thought out. Too strong of a spirit is possibly counter productive, just as having too large of an engine in a car which is intended for road use can be a waste of technology, and perhaps a too powerful force to always keep under control. Familiar spirits are often best, and although I say that in the context of spirits who are familiar to the user, the spirits known as familiars, often in animal form, are also good choices as these are familiar in the former case as well as the latter.

Some Aetherial spirits may become associated with a specific task, as with the other elemental spirits. More often, a spirit with whom the pratitioner has formed a bond will be called for many tasks. The Art of spirit magic lies in directing the chosen spirit successfully. As I said earlier, Aetherial spirits are powerful forces which may not respond well to arrogance any more than to inept use of magic. Much of this Art lies in using symbols and resonances, as has been stressed in previous volumes of this series. In the realm of Aether, words and images have great power. The formal structure of ritual is a medium through which words and images can be focused on intent, and magic is produced and directed through these symbols of the mind expressed in Spirit. It is in the realm of Aether, also called Spirit, that directing these forces can most vehemently depend on an understanding of the nature of magical correspondences.

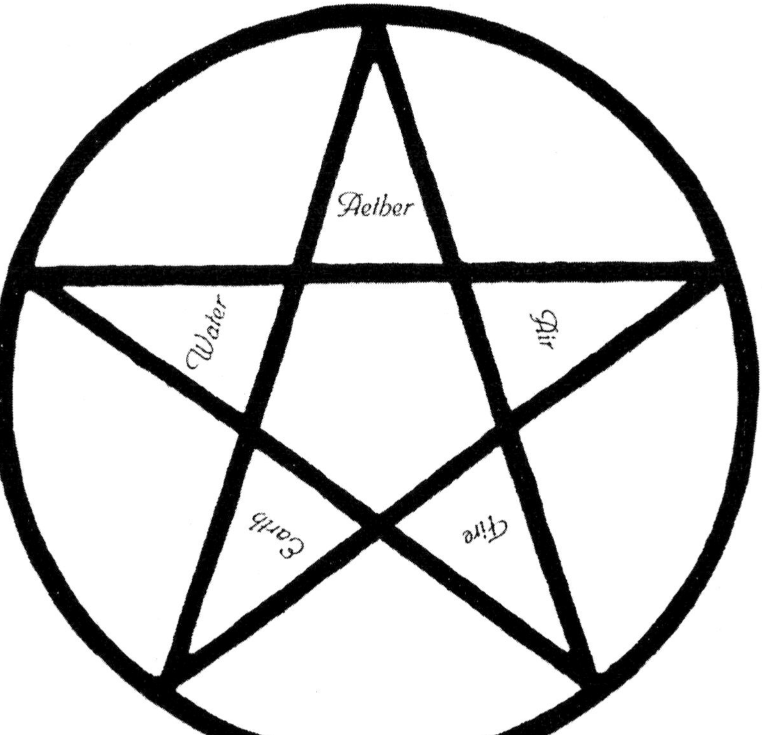
Aether
Water
Air
Earth
Fire

Chapter 8

Aetherial Correspondences

I have said in the previous volumes of this series that elemental spirits take little notice of the associations which human magicians make between the various things such as stones and planets, herbs and colours, etc. However, here in the world of pure Spirit, such things take on new meaning.

In *Spirits of the Water*, I began to explain the significance of correspondences to the subconscious and to the emotions more fully. In dealing directly with Spirit, these realms become more significant and essential to our means of communication. Spirit responds to the part of us that is of its own substance. In magic, we may use a language like Enochian to appeal to Angelic entities or symbols like magic squares to appeal to other denizens of the Aetherial world because our knowledge of these systems of communication translates directly through our own spiritual essence to that with which we wish to communicate.

The correspondences given in the previous volumes of this series take on new importance when applied to dealing with Aetherial presences, many of which overlap in nature with the elemental spirits which have been described in those volumes. The esoteric knowledge of a magician must include some degree of understanding of correspondences between one thing and another because these associations creates a nonverbal link, even if it is often combined with a verbal one, first within ourselves during ritual and then with any spirit to which we wish to transfer the information. Much of magic is done on a subconscious level. This is why The Art requires training to be effective. Mastering techniques of the subconscious is a lifelong study. Using correspondences is a simple and basic beginning to the study which is easily used in folk magic and other beginning forms of magic, but carries on into more advanced study as well. It can get a bit more complicated as one goes along, but is worth the effort of study for one who aspires to working directly with Aetherial spirits.

I mentioned the Enochian language. This is a language developed by, or channelled to depending on one's belief, Dr. John Dee. It is meant for communication with Angelic beings, and has become popular for use in a spectrum of magical systems. The study of this language is far too complicated to explain in part of a chapter of a book with a broader scope, but it is a subject worth researching and books do exist which specifically deal with it including an Enochian Dictionary. Most libraries and bookstores can order books on the subject if they are not already in stock.

Magic squares are another form of communication with the subconscious for the purpose of magical evokation. They work in a more pictorial sense, as they are a method of sigil creation. MacGregor Mathers' *Key of Solomon the King* is a good source for information on this method, but it is a simple enough system to demonstrate here as well.

A planetary square is chosen for the intended purpose, such as the square of Saturn which is;

4	9	2
3	5	7
8	1	6

or Jupiter;

```
 4  14  15   1
 9   7   6  12
 5  11  10   8
16   2   3  13
```

Notice that the sum of the numbers in any row add up to the same total, including diagonally. This will be the planetary number for that square's planet. Next, the name of a spiritual entity is chosen such as the Angels which formed much of John Dee's magical practices or demons. The letters for the names are worked out according to the basic numerology chart given in *Spirits of the Fire* such as for *Asmodeus*;

A=1
S=1
M=4
O=6
D=4
E=5
U=3
S=1

Then you basically connect the dots to create a sigil as follows;

This design is Asmodeus' Saturn sigil, which is good for giving personal insight into your own Saturnian nature. To use it, simply stare at it in meditation, preferably while in magical trance, during the day and hour of Saturn while the Moon is waxing. Planetary Hours and days are covered extensively in Arthur Edward Waite's *Book of Black Magic and of Pacts*, which is one of the older books on magic which can still often be found in libraries and goes in and out of print periodically.

Much of John Dee's correspondences of Angels is recorded in Ms. Harley 6482 in the British Library, which includes the following;

Angels presiding over the Planets:

Saturn	Zaphkiel
Jupiter	Zadkiel
Mars	Camiel
Sun	Raphael
Venus	Haniel
Mercury	Michael
Moon	Gabriel

Angel Presidents of the twelve signs:

Aries	Malchidael
Taurus	Asmodel
Gemini	Ambriel
Cancer	Muriel
Leo	Verchiel
Virgo	Hamaliel
Libra	Zuriel
Scorpio	Barbiel
Sagittarius	Advachiel
Capricorn	Hanael
Aquarius	Gambiel
Pisces	Barchiel

Twenty-Eight Angels which rule in the Twenty-Eight Mansions of the Moon:

1 Geniel	10 Ardesiel	20 Kiriel
2 Enediel	11 Nociel	21 Bethnael
3 Amnixiel	12 Abduxuel	22 Geliel
4 Azariel	13 Jazeriel	23 Requiel
5 Azariel	14 Ergodiel	24 Abrinael
6 Dirachiel	15 Ataliel	25 Aziel
7 Scheliel	16 Azeruel	26 Tagriel
8 Amnediel	17 Adriel	27 Alhoniel
9 Barbiel	18 Egibiel	28 Amnixiel
	19 Amutiel	

Four Angels of the Winds:

East   Michael
West   Raphael
North Gabriel
South Uriel, also called Nariel

Four Most Powerful Kings in command over the evil spirits:

East   Uricus
South Amaymon
West   Paymon
North Egyn

Those who are interested in pursuing Angel magic and/or Demonology more extensively will find plenty of information on these subjects with just a bit of research. Angels in particular have been enjoying a resurgence of popularity in recent years, and the plethora of books available on the subject reflect this rise in interest. Some of it becomes rather 'new age' to say the least, but the discerning researcher can find much of value by paying attention to the sources of information.

In *Spirits of the Earth*, I referred to the Alchemical concept of *First Matter*. Science has come a long way since the early Alchemists believed that all things are made up of Earth, Air, Fire and Water, yet recent discoveries since the advent of chaos science in some ways seem to have brought science full circle back to many of the ideas which originated through Alchemy. In his article *Random Reality* (New Scientist, 26 February 2000), Marcus Chown tells us that reality is based on the total randomness of the universe (a concept voiced by Peter J. Carroll long since) and that the German mathematician Gottfried Leibniz believed that reality was built from things he called *monads*, which owed their existence solely to their relations with each other. The concept that particles and objects may have existence only by relating to each other is rather significant in the area of correspondence magic, for obvious reasons. The article also describes the randomness of definitions of things in the science of physics, which depending on one's point of view may easily bring one back to defining the basic building blocks of substance by the Alchemical definitions with as much validity as the more complicated theories which abound in the scientific world today.

Keeping in mind that correspondences are a method of creating associations in the human mind between things which might not otherwise relate to each other, correspondences can easily be found between different systems or pantheons. For example, the following is a rather brilliant system of correspondences using Alchemical concepts to define the Wiccan triple Goddess associations, which has been contributed by Anton Channing (Frater M 1232), author of the *Kaos Heiroglyphica*;

Maiden = Sulphur:
Virgin goddesses are often demanding, active warrior/huntresses, such as Artemis and Athena. In the zodiacal progression, it is Aries, a cardinal (sulphur) sign which is the youngest.

Mother = Salt:
Mother goddesses are often figures of worldly power and stability. Perhaps even the Earth itself (i.e. Gaia). The power is more stable than sulphur, it is the power of security and the status quo.

Crone = Mercury:
Nearing death, the crone seeks only wisdom. She is gaining knowledge of the psychopomp (i.e. Mercury) in preparation for death, transcendance of the duality of existence. Because of this knowledge and wisdom of death she possesses, she is a formidable character. A mutable sign, Pisces, is considered the eldest sign of the zodiac.

Frater M has left us to realize for ourselves that salt represents the fixed signs of the zodiac, an obvious association. Salt has often been used to represent things which are stable such as in the phrase "the salt of the Earth".

Correspondences are necessary for mental imagery, both in words and pictures, which creates an avenue through which we can communicate on a magical level with both our deeper selves and with the spiritual essences which we seek to know and to allow into our magical practices. There are many, many more ways in which things may correspond with each other, and in the end we must learn to create these associations for ourselves from those materials which we have to hand. The correspondences listed in old books of magic are useful in that they teach us the methods by which this system works and can be used 'as is' for many purposes, but in the end they become dated and less relevant to modern magicians and witches who seek magic in new ways and methods which allow the differing paradigms of thought which develop to be incorporated into the magic itself.

Once the methods of correspondence are mastered and thoroughly understood, they can be created, re-created, and applied to any number of magical systems or practices. Knowing the ways in which magic works on the deepest levels of gnosis is at the heart of becoming an effective magician. There are many paths to magic. One is not 'better' than another per se, only more effective for one person while another method may work better for someone else. No knowledge is wasted, all methods are valid so long as they work.

To apply correspondences to the realm of the magic of Spirit, one is well advised to seek information from all quarters, even those which seem outdated and redundant. There is still value in old lace. When we move into the area of creating thought-form elementals of Spirit, the value of old knowledge becomes inestimable. The reasons for this can become all too apparent for those who delve into this area unprepared. Let the reader be warned.

Chapter 9

Aetherial Thought-Forms

Creating an artificial elemental in the realm of Spirit can be a tricky business, especially for those who have been indoctrinated into a religious system at an early age, yet is very much the stuff of wizardry in the oldest sense of the practice of magic. Thought-forms, as I have explained in earlier volumes of this series, are created out of the mind and emotions of the magician. The realm of emotions in particular can be very difficult to direct effectively and often operates at the edge of balance, where an archetypal image may well push the equilibrium of control out of the magician's hands if such an image has powerful associations in the mind which carries residual programming.

Thought-forms which take the forms of archetypal Angels and demons for example, as is depicted in many of the older 'horror' films, can sway the emotive poise of one who has had a Christian childhood, as so many who read this series will have done, with sufficient effect that the magician can easily slip into awe of the familiar image, all but forgetting that it is only a depiction and that the spirit itself is one of the magician's own making.

This is a danger of which one should always remain aware when creating Aetherial thought-forms. It is essential to remember that it is only a thought-form, a part of oneself and within one's own control. Maintaining that control will

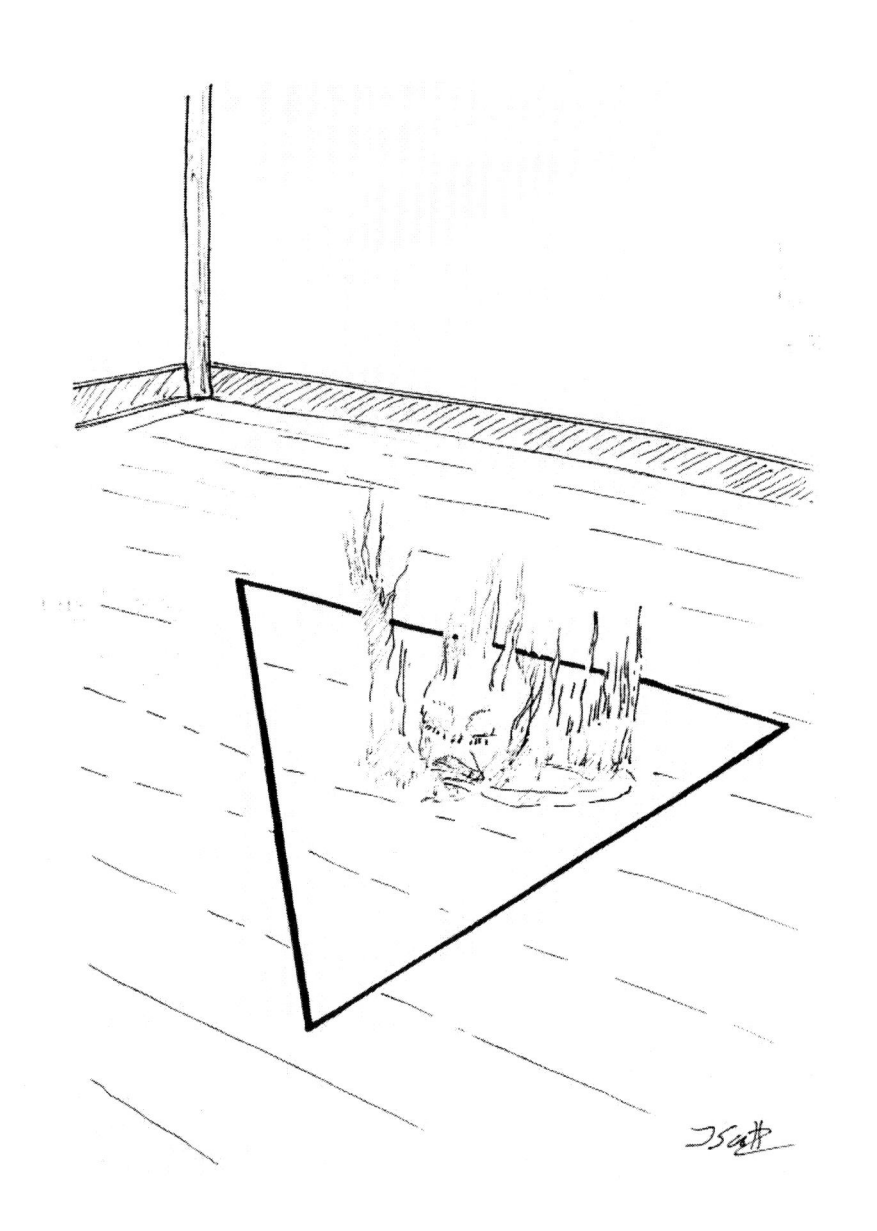

depend on the efficacy of this belief. Those who are unable to maintain this paradigm of belief are best advised to avoid this area of magic.

In *Spirits of the Earth*, I explained that thought-forms are different from natural elementals primarily by the separation of 'being' and 'purpose'. In nature, an elemental is spawned by the need for 'being', although it may also have purpose, as a spiritual entity to inhabit or care for the requisite element. A thought-form is created by a magician, usually for a specific purpose. There are incidents where a thought-form may be formed accidentally in response to a need for purpose as well, but in both cases the entity is very much a reality and must be properly directed in order to accomplish its purpose and eventually dissipate or be reabsorbed by the source at completion.

Austin Osman Spare's concept of 'Free Belief', which was briefly described in *Spirits of the Water*, can be a very valuable tool in dealing with thought-forms of any kind, especially those of the Aetherial realm. The ability to believe or not believe equally in the existence of a spiritual entity at will can very effectively determine its existence or non-existence, provided that this existence is only being effected by a single magician and not being strengthened by others. Keeping one's Aetherial entities to oneself, even those which take on the attributes of deity, retains absolute governance of its continued existence, and yet sharing a favoured servitor with others can strengthen its attributes into more solid existence which may have value as well. This is a decision that one must make in each individual situation.

Repeating what I have said in all of the volumes of this series, a thought-form, of any kind, can and will behave independently, often to the perturbation of its own creator. Any of them might easily get out of hand if very strict parameters are not set up for them at inception. A fair bit of magical experience is highly recommended before attempting this area of magic at all, and even then personal supervision by someone with sufficient experience is a very good idea. Too often, a young magician will read a few books, including some sensationalist novels, and then decide to conjure up the most formidable servitor they can conceive of for some minor purpose, which begs for a lesson in 'be careful what you wish for'. A large percentage of these simply fail to produce anything at all as the experience level of the neophyte simply isn't up to the operation, but there are always some, especially if they have a natural affinity for magic, who may succeed. This can lead to a test of the magician's nerve, wit and defensive abilities which might be a valuable magical lesson, but there are more desirable methods for gaining such lessons which are far less of a threat to the neophyte's sanity and well-being.

I explained in *Spirits of the Earth* that a thought-form which is conjured into the form of a demon is likely to behave like one, and that creating such a spirit into a more agreeable form may well make the difference in whether it will perform in the manner which one actually had in mind. It is well worth considering the nature of the purpose to which one plans to put an Aetherial thought-form before developing any preconceived ideas as to its form. A demon may well serve the specific purpose, but then again an archetypal fairy may do as well without the connotation picked up from watching *Fantasia* and a couple of Dennis Wheatley or Lovecraft inspired films, which most of us have at some time or another. On the other hand, an image of a horrific demon set as the guardian of one's Temple or sacred magical space may have very effective results on an intruder if the image is sufficiently contained by the resident magician. One must consider the options.

Such a guardian is one purpose that an Aetherial thought-form might be put to. Another is a particularly difficult healing spell, where divine intervention is called for. Aetherial spirits may be useful for intensive divinations where the Akashic records themselves must be consulted, or for a whale of a protection spell for the ardent paranoid or genuinely endangered. Aetherial thought-forms may be put to a full spectrum of tasks, but the point is that one might be going over the top in using such a spirit for most purposes. A lesser entity may well be more appropriate, and I advise strongly against prosperity spells of any kind where Aetherial spirits are concerned. The ingrained attitudes which we all carry about material wealth are such that even a servitor of one's own making might easily be insulted by such an attempt, although an Earth servitor can be happily set to achieve specific material goals.

Aether is of Spirit, and it is transmutation of one's own spirit which is most appropriate to this realm. An Aetherial thought-form may be conjured to fill the place of Holy Guardian Angel in Crowlian terms, or a similar sort of overseeing spirit of one's magical and/or spiritual development. Whatever purpose is set for the intended spirit, it should be well defined before beginning any operation to attain its existence.

Obviously quarter guardians would involve spirits of the basic four elements whether they were natural or thought-form entities, but Aether is more appropriate to deity or an overall ruling spirit if it is to be used at all. Most people who choose deity representations will align with a known deity from a chosen pantheon. A smaller percentage of those who choose to include deity on their Altar will choose a form from mythology or even fiction. There are a select few who will actually create an original deity form, and this is where a thought-form can be very appropriate.

Many years ago, I was introduced to the cult of Azo. A particular group of very serious magicians with a rather

Discordian inclination to their magic created their own god, Azo. The representation of Azo was and still is a toy mechanical black and white cow, one of those which walks a few steps and then stops to 'moo' a few times before continuing on its irregular path. Into this representation was conjured the spirit of Azo.

This sounds a bit silly, yet it was very effective and the magicians are some I knew well and still respect highly. Azo participates in spells and has been seen walking along and mooing his blessings in many very intense rituals, often involving ecstatic dance. Nobody ever steps on Azo. He is the sacred cow, in all the seriousness of deity, and repeated rituals have only increased the aura of divinity which permeated Azo very thoroughly before I first met him.

Creating an Aetherial Thought-Form

The method for creating an Aetherial thought-form is very much like that which is described in the previous volumes of this series. The primary difference is that there is no need for a connection to a physical element, as we are now dealing with pure Spirit. However, one should not take for granted the importance of Spirit in the operation. Such an entity will be created from a combined force of the wellspring of Spirit with the magician's own spirit, and consequently will take much energy from the magician(s) who generate its existence.

As specified earlier, the purpose should be well thought out before beginning. Alternatives should also be considered, this is not a daily magic or a minor ritual. Having made the decision, the parameters must be clearly set. Examples of how to do this for specific purposes will be included in the appendix. A physical representation of the spirit may be provided, or it may be created in pure Spirit within a contained space.

A Temple setting is recommended for this operation. The formality of ritual lends itself well to dealing with the realm of Spirit in this manner. A proper opening to the ritual should include a thorough banishing of the work space at the very beginning. Residual energies could be very disruptive if left to become 'impurities' in this form of spirit. A statement of intent for the creature followed by a form of spirit infusion is the basic formulae for this purpose. The statement should be *very* specific as to the intended purpose of the entity, and should include a plan for its ultimate predestination. Circling the central spot where the spirit is to be contained during formation is an ideal way of using spiral energies to give 'life' to its form, perhaps using some form of dance in conjunction with an exhaustive chant of creation. Again, specific examples will be included in the appendix.

As with any similar ritual, any feeling of foreboding or simply 'wrongness' in the situation should be reacted to by aborting the ritual and immediately performing a thorough banishing. This should be done even if only one member of an involved group is experiencing difficulty and everyone else is fine, as the distress of that one member will translate into the finished product and as a weak link in a chain, will form a weakness in the overall result which could be potentially dangerous in a major operation.

As with other thought-forms, once the entity is created it must be released and then the ritual should be properly closed and a very exhaustive banishing performed. This is no time to be lazy and do short versions of standard banishings. If standard forms are used, do the whole rite. Residual energies in the realm of Spirit are not to be ignored. If there is a lack in the feeling of completion which generally follows a ritual well done, banish again.

Then of course, the thought-form must be sustained until completion of its purpose.

Sustaining An Aetherial Thought-Form

All thought-forms exist on Aetherial energy, generally provided by their creators as well as absorbed from other available resources. A thought-form begins from the substance inputted to its formation and then continues to draw from the original source, but over time it begins to absorb any loose bits of sustaining force which it may encounter. This is why the longer a thought-form continues to exist, the more independent it may become. It can develop survival instincts as well as autonomy.

A thought-form which is sent to perform a specific task should therefore be given a time limit as well as a plan for reabsorption. The clever magician will also allow for dealing with any bits of influence which the entity might have picked up in its travels either by a purification ritual before reabsorbing the original entity form, or through assimilation if the magician is able to turn such random influences into added personal strength. This is not a trick for beginners.

Guardians and artificial deities will obviously be sustained for long periods of time and subject to many variations of influence, therefore some parameters must be carefully set at their inception. A Temple guardian may be largely containable, but any fluctuations in the group population will still bring potential change. These are things which must be considered when making the decision to create such an entity.

Ironically, Azo, as a Chaos god, is able to balance the influences of any number of participants in his fluctuating ritual appearances specifically because he is a god of Chaos, and therefore quite content to juggle a plethora of variations in his sustaining energies which are transmuted into his 'blessings' by the very nature of chaotic bifurcation. An impressive Alchemical feat for a mechanical toy turned servitor!

Repeated rituals are the best source of sustenance for a deity servitor. The form of 'worship' will form much of the continuing character of the entity, which is something to keep in mind. Dramatic forms of sustenance will naturally lead to dramatic demands from the deity, so think on. A large degree of judgement is required when dealing with thought-forms.

Whatever the purpose, thought-forms can be a beneficial addition to the magical practices of a sensible magician or witch. Aetherial thought-forms specifically are not to be used lightly as I have tried to emphasis, but one of the safest areas in which to deal with these powerful entities is in the realm of serious divination. Just be sure that you really do want to know.

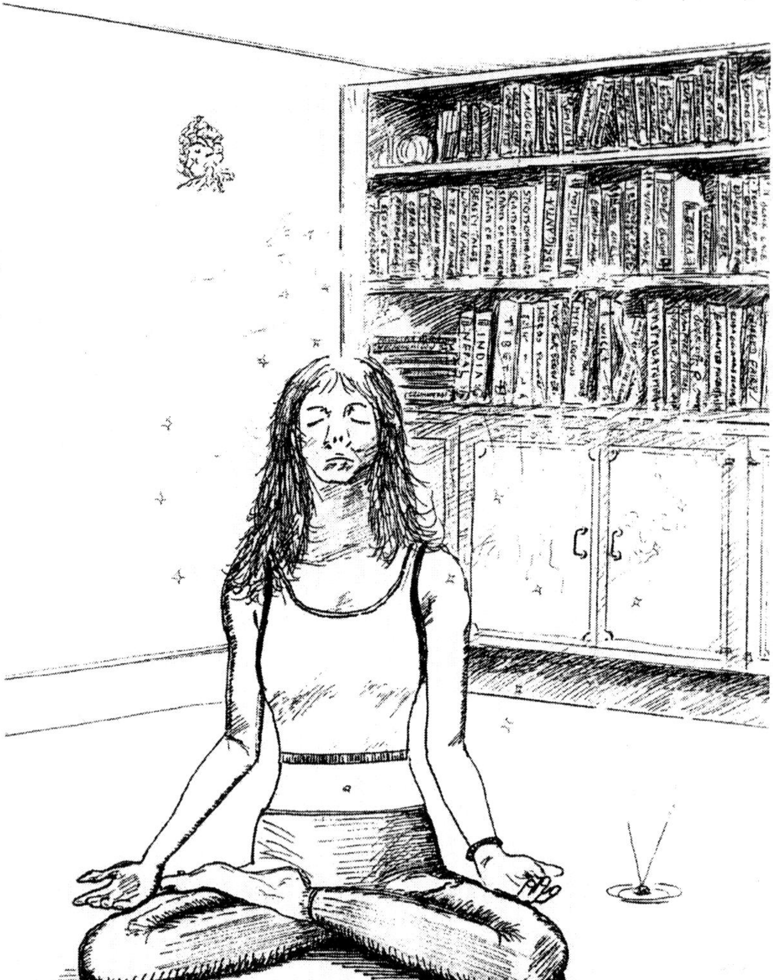
INDIA
NEPAL
TIBET

Chapter 10

Divination With Aetherial Spirits

Bringing spirits of any form into divination immediately addresses the world of Spirit, or Aether. Such things as mediumship, the use of ouija and common prayer are all direct avenues to Spirit. Aetherial divination may use items, such as in ouija, which are of other elements but it is the invoking or discourse with spirits which defines the method as 'of Aether'. This may include our own spirits, as some have been known to seek guidance or information through astral travel or by consulting the 'higher self'.

Methods for consulting one's own higher spirit, by whatever name one may choose to call it, can be found in many religious and magical disciplines. Eastern religions teach various forms of meditation and yoga which provide very good avenues to this accession. Tribal societies are known to travel in Spirit through the use of natural drugs, such as peyote among the Mexican shamen and some more complicated mixtures in other cultures such as the Voudon and Santeria religions, and even substances more familiar to Western culture such as the famous Witches flying ointment. The trouble of course with the use of such drugs is that they are not accessible to those who are not acquainted with the relevant culture or the priests (by whatever name) among them, who must be carefully trained to mix complicated and potentially lethal substances. These are not things for dabbling.

One's own spirit can be accessed by many other methods. Over the past four decades, Western society has experienced rather a lot of social change which has included adapting Eastern and tribal methods of meditation and trance to achieve spiritual states, and some small groups have developed original methods for accessing the 'higher self'. One such is the use of cut-ups, which is a simple technique and can lead to amazing results. It is a word association approach. In the original and most basic form, magazines are cut into pieces of text and mixed into a container (a hat or bowl works well) and bits of paper are chosen at random and put into a sequential order, then read as sentences of a message. This will, on the surface, appear to result in nonsense prose, but within the randomness of the word order the higher mind will find relevant messages to the intent or concern of the reader.

In a similar fashion, many other forms of divination can be used to access the subconscious or superconscious areas of the mind. A basic tarot reading may be of Earth in its usual form, but the random choosing of tarot cards and interpretation thereof opens a path to deeper parts of the mind which can look beyond the basic interpretations of the cards, and make use of the random element of such divination methods. Randomness, after all, is the basic structure of the universe from whence we all are created, and relates to everyday life far more than many people are consciously aware. From this point of consciousness, the seeker may find answers to whatever questions are of concern, or they may wish to seek the aid of an outside spirit.

Specifically conjuring a spirit to help with divination can sometimes be a useful thing to do. In the previous volumes of this series, I have suggested ways in which elemental spirits may be applied toward various forms of divination. While some people choose to directly consult some form of guardian or guide spirit which accesses the inner self much as already described, others may choose to petition a god form or other spirit according to their personal belief structure, who will answer questions through inner illumination. Whatever the philosophical or theological beliefs of the reader may be, I would advise careful selection in the form of Aetherial spirit one chooses to consult for divination purposes. Many forms of spirits are known for intentionally giving incorrect information, or in some cases for giving correct information in a way which may cause distress. This has been well publicised in the use of ouija, which is a divination form which can attract a fairly random spirit response.

Spirits, like fairies, can be playful rather than malicious, but the result is still confusion. For those who do not have a fair amount of experience of working with spirits, usually I would advise common forms of divination such as tarot cards or runes, which provide a solid medium for readings, although they are still open to misinterpretation, especially when reading for oneself. A favoured spirit form may be called on to assist the accuracy of the reading, usually a god form or guiding spirit which is known to the reader.

Most people know that divining for oneself is often difficult, as it is too easy to interpret whatever medium one uses as one would choose to believe. Regular consultation with a 'higher' spirit form can help to maintain objectivity, even when one believes that the spirit form is a prototype for one's own 'higher self'.

As I explained in *Spirits of the Earth*, asking a spirit for guidance during a divination can often take the form of a simple petition or prayer. One of the most impressive well known rune masters I have ever met regularly consults the Norse deities before doing a divination in order to determine the suitability of the proposed spell. The deity is chosen according to the intent of the spell itself, although he does have a few favourites. Similarly, one may learn to attach spiritual significance to an object, icon or specific place in relation to divination work.

Someone who regularly visits a special place of some sort may wish to invoke or evoke the spirit of the location to guide a meditation, or one may have a personal spirit who can be invoked by name. This can be done internally, or through a ritualistic invocation such as, "*I call the spirit* (name) *to come to me and guide my thoughts and visions, and to show me the answer to* (question)". Words, as I have said many times in this series, are a matter of individual choice and are likely to be more effective when they express feeling rather than being read from a book (including the books in this series) as if they were some arcane magical formulae. However, using the same invocation repeatedly will create an affinity with the wording itself which can be very effective for recurrent use.

Attuning an object to an Aetherial spirit is a bit different than doing so with spirits of the basic four elements. Any object is likely to be effected by a spirit of the object itself, most often an Earth spirit. However, spirits easily blend with each other in the right circumstances. Religious icons are probably the most common form of objects which attract the attention of Aetherial spirits. Such spirits are not actually attached to the object in the way that the resident Earth spirit may be, but are attracted by the association made with it by the human supplicant. Regular observances to an icon or a group of icons will attract the sort of spirit essence which is associated with it in the mind of the magician or petitioner, although this can also be effected by associations made to the same spirit form by others past or present.

This can of course be avoided by creating servitor entities with objects which do not carry associations with any familiar archetypes, but in general many people find that god or goddess associations provide a stronger source of clarity. Furthermore, I personally find that a group of icons creates a more balanced energy than adherence to a single god form. Once upon a time, I set up an Altar with the dual aspects of Sekhmet and Hathor from the Egyptian pantheon represented. These goddesses had been instrumental in a major spell which I felt was sufficiently significant to construct an Altar in order to show my appreciation for their assistance toward my purpose, which had been accomplished far beyond my essential requirements. The duality of the two goddesses was soon further balanced by the gift of a Bast statue from a friend, which seemed to add just the right touch for an Egyptian goddess Altar. When my life changed to include a new relationship, I immediately became aware of the need for a male entity to balance the sexual polarity of the Altar. This was quickly followed by the sudden availability of a rather nice statue of Horus in a friend's shop.

The Altar was more than a simple monument to an accomplished purpose, but became a sort of shrine to the attributes of the chosen god/dess forms and a pathway of access to divinatory insights. Attuning to icon images is easily done through any sort of daily observance. In the case of my Egyptian Altar, it was the lighting of a sandalwood incense cone every morning, which also served to scent the house nicely. The dedication of an Altar or single icon can also be done through formal ritual, using an opening and closing as desired, but this is a matter of personal choice. One does not have to supplicate oneself to a religious belief in the god/dess forms of such an Altar or pantheon in order to attune to the energies represented by it. As a Chaos Magician, I do not believe in specific gods or goddesses in their personifications, but for the purpose of a specific spell can adopt their attributes into my belief system for the duration of a spell in order to access specific qualities of the chosen deity. My choice to further emulate these specific entities for a year afterwards was a tribute to the level of success of the magic which had been performed with their reinforcement. An act of appreciation can only facilitate one's relationship with Spirit.

The nature of Spirit is such that the boundaries between one's own spirit and an external spirit source are by nature difficult to determine. Divination with a representation of deity or other spirit is very subjective. Some may offer petitions to the icon, while others simply sit in front of the representation(s) and wait for impressions. It is important to learn techniques for clearing the mind with this sort of divination, which will allow one's own thought processes to operate most efficiently as well as leaving room for any Aetherial messages. Basic exercises in meditation and breathing techniques are highly recommended for anyone who wishes to work with Spirit in any form. The techniques of Asana and Pranayama yoga are ideal for the beginner, and form the basis for many magical systems despite their Eastern origins. Asana is the act of stillness. One sits in a comfortable position for a period of time, beginning with only five minutes at a sitting, and clears the mind. This is more difficult than it sounds. Thoughts intrude, the body naturally seeks to move around, and a real effort of concentration is required at first simply to sit still and control the influx of 'noise' which occurs normally in the thought process. Some versions of this method are made easier by concentrating the thoughts on an image of some sort. It can also be made easier by directing the thoughts to simultaneous Pranayama, which is a technique of breathing. Breath in slowly to the count of four, stop the breath without actually holding and locking it for the count of four, then release slowly to the count of four and wait again for the count of four before breathing in again. Focusing on the count can keep the mind busy. For more detailed instructions of these and other basic techniques, the reader is advised to read *Liber Null and Psychonaut* by Peter J Carroll, which is the best single book which I have personally found which describes these and other techniques which are common to most magical systems.

It goes without saying that respect should always be shown to elemental spirits of any kind, but especially to spirits of the Aether. Those who are of the realm of Spirit itself can be extremely helpful in the arts of divination or even in giving good advice freely without having been asked, but they cannot be demanded of, and any attempt to command spirits by force is unlikely to obtain a good result, despite what some old books (mostly fantasy horror) may say about commanding demons to give up bits of information in response to specific arcane phrases. This is the stuff of old black and white films, real spirits are not so easily submissive to human control. In the world of Spirit, there is much knowledge to be had if one but realizes the ease with which one may gain the willing support of Spirit itself, in whatever form it may choose to manifest.

It is in Aether that the elements come together to form a whole. As a prism separates light into bands of colour which mixed together form the manifestation of white light, we as spiritual beings form a medium through which the diversity of spiritual energies which are represented by the various elements can come together into a gestalt Spirit, a realm of diversity and unity in that very diversity which forms the basis of our very natures as spiritual beings. We are magic, and in nature is evidence of magic at work at every level. It is our free choice to learn to understand magic, and in that understanding we find the road to knowledge of the future and the present, as well as lessons learned in the past. It is in Aether, the element of Spirit, where the whole of our nature is realized. We can divine through the divine if you will, divination through understanding of divinity. The road to Spirit, whether it is for conjuration or for seeking knowledge, will still lead to knowledge, and in the practice of magic and divination we become better able to know the unknown, and to sense those methods which will bring us to spiritual knowledge including knowledge of the future and the feeling which accompanies such knowledge, once we learn to trust our 'sixth sense' or intuition, which are only terms for knowledge of that which we know from a spiritual understanding rather than from material facts.

The ability is there for all of us. Self love and self trust are the beginning of spiritual love and trust, and it is in that trust of self and Spirit where divination of any form becomes a path to certain knowledge. Spirit permeates every aspect of one's life once one becomes open to some form of it. Knowledge gained through divination simply follows the acceptance of the magical life, where methods of divination are an acceptable form of spirituality, and the methods which one chooses become just that, a matter of free choice.

Chapter 11

Living With Aetherial Spirits

Spirit permeates our lives, regardless of our beliefs of what form it may take. Even those who do not believe in extant spirits have a belief in their own essence. Those sad few who believe that even this dissipates into nothing at death have to cling steadfastly to their dependence on this belief, casting off the bombardment of evidence of Spirit which assaults their senses through the experiences of others, and sometimes themselves, yet cannot be pinned down or bottled for scrutiny.

There is far more to Spirit than belief alone. Spirit exists as the motivating force behind life itself, and yet its existence occurs in a realm that the average person does not usually see or touch in the tactile sense. It cannot be measured or dissected. Belief is an odd thing, something which varies from one person to another, and yet accommodates the diversity of beliefs which occur among many different people.

Some have learned, like Austin Osman Spare, that belief can actually shape reality, not just perception. And yet perception is the basis of the freedom of belief which allows this magic to happen. To choose to perceive that something is other than it may otherwise seem to be, is the beginning step to creating a change in the reality. The limits of magic are like the limits of the spiritual realm, unknowable. To test boundaries will

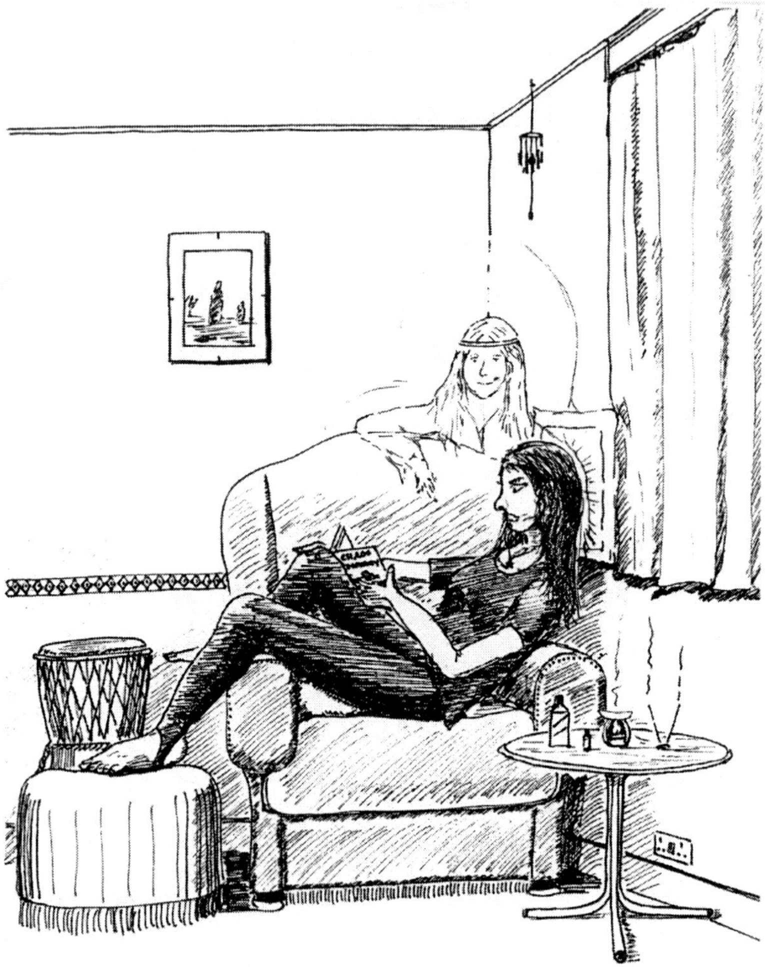

bring randomly divergent results. There are no solid empirical answers in Spirit.

Those who pick up this book will likely already know Spirit in some form. The Aetherial spirits within our perceptions may vary according to each individual's understanding of their nature, such is the very nature of Spirit. And such is the nature of Aether, that the magic takes many forms, individual to each of us who partake of its currents. There is no right way or wrong way to perform magic, only methods which are successful or unsuccessful, and these will be different for one person or another. The only real test of a magical method or system is "*Does it work?*"

Spirit is of nature, as it is of magic. The magic in nature is accessible through many paths, yet has a consistency which may be understood through an open mind, and an open heart. All who partake of magic, and therefore move within the world of Aether, have an element of common experience, although the ways and methods for touching Spirit may diverge greatly.

Knowing the spirits of Aether, whether we understand them as projections of inner Spirit or as separate entities in whatever form, awakens our own magical potential and the very power of Spirit which is accessible to us all. As I said in *Spirits of the Earth*, those of us who are drawn to the world of magic owe it to ourselves to learn about the nature of Spirit. It is our own spiritual nature which draws us into magic to begin with.

Those who come to Spirit for its own sake and seek not magic, may have to redefine the word 'magic', because they will find magic within the transformation of Spirit. Nature is of Spirit, and nature is naturally chaotic, and very much a thing of magic. The realm of Spirit creates the magic of life and of hope, enthusiasm and endurance. All of the qualities of humankind which are referred to commonly as 'having spirit' are closely akin to that which we think of as the higher definition of Spirit, that which is ethereal, or Aetherial. In Aether, we find that we come full circle in a quest for answers which always seems to find more questions. The answers exist, but not as we expect to find them. Answers to questions of Spirit are as transmutative and flexible as the Aether itself.

Addressing Spirit directly is a more intense experience than much of the spirit contact which occurs closer to the individual elements. Pure Spirit is intoxicating in its absolute clarity, and the immersion into the world of Spirit transforms us, melding the nature of our own spirits within the force of nature and magic which is our birthright as living creatures.

Whatever form of practice we choose to employ in addressing Spirit, the ultimate goal is the Alchemical self-transformation which we seek whether consciously or subconsciously, every time we seek contact with the spirits of the Aether.

Appendix

As with the previous volumes of this series, the spells in the appendix are samples only. With Aetherial spirits in particular, the forms that spells may take are many and varied, and what works for one person may be very different than what appeals to another. Belief comes into it with the element of Spirit. For some, prayer is the only way to approach these spirits. For others, evoking spirits into a triangle on the Temple floor is the way to go. For the purposes of the series, I will offer spells which fit the format which has occurred in the previous volumes, but this is not an indication that it is the only way that I would deal with the element of Spirit and its various spirit forms myself. Those who read my other books may find very different methods within them, depending on context.

Spells in this series are offered as models for beginners or those who have need of a structure for delving into a different area of magic than they have done before, or for those who are looking for a different perspective than whatever they have worked with to date. Magic is not limited to a few methods, but is approachable from many different paths. The spirits do not listen to only one voice.

What works for you will become apparent in time and with practice. Elemental spirits and 'higher' spirits alike will respond best to what comes from the heart, rather than to anything which is read from a page. Follow your own will and inclinations when choosing methods and you will find the words with the meanings you want to express, as you set your own spirit free to work magic with the spirits of the Aether.

Opening An Aetherial Ritual

In the realm of Aether, opening a formal ritual is a matter of attuning oneself to the spiritual entity form to which one wishes to address oneself. For some people the entire ritual consists of prayer, but for others, I offer here a magician's approach. The process of making the shift into ritual consciousness begins by gathering the representations with which one chooses to adorn the Altar. These may include practical working tools as well as icons or just decorations. Some magical traditions hold that it is appropriate to bath before ritual. This is a rather good representation of purification, and can be done as a proper bath or symbolically by washing ones hands and splashing a bit of Water around elsewhere. Then without speaking, one begins to gather the items for the Altar.

The type of spirit one wishes to invoke or evoke will strongly effect the choices of items used. In general, some combination of the following are appropriate;

1. Representations of the four directions and/or elements, traditionally a Pentacle for Earth, a Wand for Air, an Athame or Sword for Fire (these last two may be reversed) and a Chalice for Water.

2. Representations of the Alchemical elements, i.e. Salt, Sulphur and Mercury (Mercury itself is liquid and hard to come by, as well as extremely toxic. Thermometers often contain it, so if you can find one that isn't too kitchy, it serves as an adequate representation).

3. Something symbolic of the deity or spirit form. Statues or pictures of gods and goddesses, fairies, Angels or daemonic creatures, or dressing up oneself as vampire, fairy, etc. for invokation purposes.

4. Basic decorations such as candles and candle holders in appropriate colours and designs, flowers, or generally decorative or symbolic items which have meaning for the practitioner.

I personally like to have a central focal point for most rituals. This may be a specific candle, an incense burner, an icon, or any number of things depending on the purpose of the ritual. If I were evoking a deity for example, I would probably centre an icon of that deity but place it such that an incense burner could be immediately in front of it as I face the Altar, so that I may make offerings to the deity through that medium. From there I would place items according to usage, rather like properly setting a dinner table. I tend to place the Athame on the left, and the Wand on the right. The Pentacle would probably have the incense burner sitting on it. A chalice would be slightly out of the way for libation later in the ritual, probably far left, next to the icon. If I'm planning to bless Water with Salt, the two containers for them would also be slightly left of centre and far enough back to be out of the way. Opposite the Chalice on the right may be a plate of cakes, further balanced by any other items chosen for the Altar. Candles, unless they are central for the purpose, are usually placed as far back as possible on each side to avoid flame hazards and knocking over. Alchemical representations are more likely to be laid out in front of the central point, bringing them to more conscious attention. All of this can vary greatly of course. One ritual I did some time ago focused rather a lot on candle colour symbolism, so the Altar consisted of a very few items placed centrally on the Pentacle and the two candles placed on either side of it. The whole set up can be as simple or as elaborate as one wishes.

Having set up the Altar, any preliminaries such as calling quarters which the magic user feels are required can be done. As a Chaos Magician myself, I do not usually call quarters unless I am working directly with the basic four elemental creatures in some manner, and prefer to perform a simple banishing (to clear ritual space) and launch directly into addressing whatever spirit form that I intend to work with on the Aetherial plane, but I am aware that some traditions require that these observances are made for any ritual, so they fit in well between the 'quieting' which comes of arranging the Altar, and the direct invokation or evokation of the desired spirit form.

In the previous volumes of this series, I have suggested sample wordings to use for opening rituals to the basic elementals. This is much more difficult with Aether as the spirit forms and purposes differ more radically. The words really must be tailored to the spirit and the purpose. There is, however, a natural progression which is demonstrated in slight variations in the examples given in the other *Spirits of the Elements* books. The banishing or calling of the quarters is performed, then the spirit is addressed in some way such as, "*I call upon* (name of spirit, the spirits of..., the god or goddess, etc.) *to come to me and aid that which I seek to do*, (name purpose in detail). From there you can make offerings, promises (careful with this one!) or explanation as to why your purpose is just. Some take a more aggressive approach and justify the purpose "*because it is my Will.*" This attitude works better with internal magic than in addressing Aetherial spirits who are likely to have a substantial Will of their own, but if the belief of the magician is that all external spirits are projected by their own spiritual essence, then they are likely to be working with just such a spirit and the imperious attitude may be well placed.

Aether And The Quarters

Those who do call quarters will often recognize the fifth element by calling deity last. Most often, after facing the appropriate directions and calling each element according to the specific tradition, the practitioner will return to the beginning point or to the centre, and there call god and goddess or whatever deity form is chosen. Those who are working with the sample spells in this series rather than another known tradition may wish to use words for this position something like, "*I call upon the spirits of the Aether, the deities and pure spirits, to witness* (my/our) *rites and to bring the purity of Spirit into* (my/our) *magic. Let it be so.*" (or "*so mote it be.*")

Closing An Aetherial Ritual

Closing an Aetherial spirit ritual can be done by many methods according to the structure of the ritual and chosen tradition of the practitioner, but emphasis should be put on some form of banishing. Calling pure spirit entities and then leaving residual forces lying around is not a good idea at all. Sometimes, a ritual is closed with just a banishing, such as the Greater Pentagram Ritual which is described in Peter J. Carroll's *Liber Null*. This is actually a very effective method, as is banishing with laughter.

Bringing a ritual to a finish is like bringing a story to a conclusion, it runs most smoothly if the ending wraps up the beginning, bringing the action full circle. If the wording of the closing reflects that of the opening, a form of continuity is maintained which brings with it a feeling of completion, which is desirable in this situation.

Closing a ritual which is modelled on the suggestions in this section may be done with a simple wording such as "*I thank you now* (name of spirit, the spirits of..., the god or goddess, etc.) *for coming to me and attending my ritual to aid that which I seek to do,* (name purpose in detail). *I release you now to the realm of Spirit, to complete that which we have begun.*"

If quarters have been used, then it may work well to close each quarter and then finish in the centre or at the Altar with something like, "*I thank the spirits of the Aether, the deities and pure spirits, for witnessing* (my/our) *rites and for bringing the purity of Spirit into* (my/our) *magic. Return now to your realm of Spirit, and let the magic be done in that realm, so that it may manifest in the material world. Let it be so.*" (or "*so mote it be.*")

The Middle Bit

As I have stated in the previous volumes of this series, the 'middle bit' of the ritual may actually comprise the entire operation. Not all purposes require a formal opening and closing. Prayer rituals for example, are often done spontaneously although they can also incorporate separate beginning and ending passages. This can be observed in most Christian churches where the prayer rituals are participatory. The clergyman will announce the beginning of the ritual with a statement, often as simple as "*Let us pray*", and will close the prayer ritual with an additional passage of his own, marking the boundaries of that segment of the service.

Pagan and magical rituals may also happen spontaneously, or not require formalized openings and closings, but will usually lend themselves well to some form of simple banishing which can be incorporated into the 'end of the middle', in the form of a statement of completion such as "*Let it be so*" or "*so mote it be*".

The magic user must make the decision as to whether these separate elements need be used. In the meantime, it is the middle portion of the ritual which defines its purpose and forms the magic to be employed. As always, I stress that original rituals created for each specific purpose are most effective. Reading something from a book is a starting point, not the act of an accomplished magician. The rituals which follow are intended as examples, to provide a format for beginners or those who wish to absorb another magician's 'style'. They are not even representative of my own style of magic so much as a generic blueprint for generally Pagan practices. Use them, adapt them, and ultimately devise your own style of ritual. Then you will feel the real magic involved in dealing with the spirits of Aether, the element of Spirit itself.

'Cleansing' A New Home

When moving into a new home, chances are that there will be some sort of 'feel' to the house or flat which is effected by many factors, including the previous inhabitants. It can be very useful to clear away old energies to be replaced by your own influences. This isn't always strictly necessary. My last flat had such a nice feel to it that I never did this in the entire time I lived there. I simply added my own effects to that which was already there.

However, in most instances of moving into a new home I find it desirable to perform a simple cleansing. One must remember that if a space is cleared, it creates a void which will be filled, and therefore part of the ritual must include some provision for filling this empty space. The first very simple ritual I ever did for this purpose was so perfectly effective that I have stuck pretty close to the original formula ever since. I use a glass candle holder which has the capacity to hold Water in the base, thereby giving me access to Fire and Water, a traditional medium for blessings. It can also be easy to incorporate Earth and Air into the ritual, as well as Aether which is directly accessible through one's own spirit which is exactly that with which one will probably want to fill the space, although infusing the influence of a preferred deity is also a possibility.

Prepare a white candle in the candle holder and fill the base with Water. If it is not possible to do this with the candleholder you are using, use a small container for the

Water, but this may be a bit awkward. The Water can be blessed with salt, incorporating Earth into the ritual at this point, and Air can be addressed through your awareness of moving through it as this is a moving ritual, no Altar will be required.

Open the ritual by your preferred method, or simply light the candle and state your purpose such as, "*I wish to clear this space of all residual energies, to be replaced by my own influence and make this truly my place.*" If other people are to live in this space as well, it may be desirable to have them participate in the ritual or to at least be present within the space. In the case of small children, it may be best to perform the ritual as they sleep and incorporate mention of them in all statements.

The next stage is most effective if the pract-itioner has some experience of magic. It is necessary to become aware of the elements and the spirits within them, as well as the feeling of Spirit, as you pick up the candle and, being careful not to spill the Water, move throughout the living space in deosil (clockwise) spiral movements while chanting something simple such as, "*I clear this space of all negativity and other spiritual presences which might interfere with* (my/our) *happiness in this place.*" Over and over again the statement must be repeated as you clear *all* areas possible within the living space. When you feel that you have covered all of the space, stop at the front door of the house or flat and begin to seal the perimeter. This is done by dipping a finger in the Water and drawing a symbol such as a solar cross or a pentagram, anything simple and meaningful to you, on the door while speaking a similar statement to the clearing chant such as, "*I seal this space from all outside influences except those which I shall invite into this place of dwelling. Let no malefic entities enter herein.*" Follow the perimeter of the living space to the next window or door, and repeat the operation. Continue to do so throughout the property until you come full circle back to the starting point (yes, this could take a while). Repeat the operation once again at the front door to seal the circle of protection.

Now sit, preferably on the floor, with the still burning candle in front of you. You should be well into 'ritual mode' by now and able to easily slip into a meditative state. Do not look into the candle flame, but over the top of it and unfocus your eyes slightly. Become aware of the entirety of the space you have just cleared and sealed, and of your own presence (and that of any other inhabitants) within it. Visualize your own spirit moving throughout the space, touching and combining with the auras of all other inhabitants, as you state that with which you would like to fill the space. This can be the spiritual presence of yourself and any other inhabitants, or you may wish to incorporate favoured deities or other spiritual guides or helpers. A basic statement can be adapted accordingly such as, "*I now fill this space with my own spirit, that this space may be of me and of nobody else.*" or "*I now fill this space with my own spirit, and those of* (name all inhabitants), *let this space be of us, and protected from all who would wish us ill.*" or "*I now fill this space with my own spirit, and those of* (other inhabitants), *let our spirits fill this space, and let the spirit of* (deity or other spirit) *dwell here among us, and be with us in protection and peace* (or any other desired qualities)."

From there, all that is required is to finish and ground yourself, but do not banish. The entire ritual was one of banishing and replacing Spirit, therefore a banishing at the end would be inappropriate. However, you will want a simple closing to mark the end of the ritual which can be as simple as repeating three times, "*Let it be so*", or can be a bit more formal if you prefer. Then ground yourself, preferably by eating something immediately and doing something mundane within the space which you have just cleansed.

Inviting An Aetherial Spirit Into The Garden, Temple Or Home

I began suggesting rituals for inviting spirits into these places in *Spirits of the Earth* and have made adaptations for Air and Water, leaving this idea out for Fire for hopefully obvious reasons. We have come full circle, as Aether forms a duality with Earth as the basis of matter/Spirit. The rituals given in *Spirits of the Earth* can be easily adapted to call or include Spirit in a garden, home or Temple spirit invokation or evokation. A specific spirit may be called, such as deity in a preferred form or the basic concept of faery, daemon realms as written about by the Findhorn community, or a guardian spirit from a chosen belief system.

To invite an Aetherial spirit to become guardian of a chosen location is much like inviting a spirit of place. One simply asks. Open the ritual according to your preferred method, then if you wish, perform some sort of blessing of the location as described above. The ritual can be as simple or as elaborate as you wish. If asking a deity form to oversee the chosen place, you may wish to perform elaborate evokation rites to connect with that spirit form, or you may choose to keep it simple and just have some bits and pieces on the Altar which are representative of the chosen spirit.

Again, using the formula from *Spirits of the Earth*, the actual invitation can be as simple as;

(for the garden):

"*Spirit of...*(or deity name), *I invite you to join my garden, to help me to care for the growing things here and to bring the balance of nature to this garden and to make of it a magical place, by the power of Earth, Air, Fire and Water, so shall it be.*" You have added Spirit by the evokation itself.

(for the Temple):

Either on it's own or after calling upon the spirits of the other elements in turn, "*I call upon the spirits of the Aether* (or a specific spirit form) *and invite them to become a part of this Temple, and those who practice within it. Let balance prevail in all workings done here, and let the spirits of the elements be as one in harmony in this place of magic.*" Add any specific qualities you wish your chosen spirit form to bring to your Temple space, and close with "*Let it be so*" or "*so mote it be*", or any other closing statement which indicated to you that you have made a statement of power.

This same formula is used for inviting the spirit into the home, inviting whichever specific qualities you wish your chosen spirit to bring into your personal space.

Inviting an Aetherial Spirit into an Object or Icon

Aetherial spirits may be invited to become associated with pretty much any object that you may wish to use to represent them. Statues are often used for deity forms, or shells to represent goddess, horns to represent gods, or items which are of significance to a specific deity. Other Aetherial spirits may also be invited into objects. One must remember, however, that in the case of Aetherial spirits, the spirit is not really a part of the object. It simply becomes associated with it.

You do not have exclusive access to a specific deity because you have a statue of it, although you may attract its attention more easily through such an object properly charged. neither do you 'trap' a fairy or daemon in an object (although there are stories of bottles....), but you may entice a specific spirit to become associated with the object so that it is likely to hear your rituals directed through the object. There is never a guarantee that they will respond in any case, but Aetherial spirits which are invited into an object are more likely to at least be aware that you are trying.

First of all, a spirit or spirit form must be chosen, then an object for representation must also be selected. This may be something you are drawn to, something you seek out, or even something which seems to 'fall into your lap' as a gift from your chosen spirit. If you first attempt to attune to the spirit itself, an appropriate object may well present itself....as if by magic!

There isn't a single catch-all ritual that can be used for all spirit forms to attune the spirit to your object. You will have to construct one according to the nature of the spirit, and of the object, and of your own chosen belief system. The basic formula offered in *Spirits of the Earth*, is again, something which can be adapted to most situations. Perform a thorough banishing and then open the ritual. Then issue an invitation such as "*I call upon* (spirit name or type) *to bring forth a spirit to inhabit this* (object)" or in the case of deity "*I call upon* (name) *to inhabit this* (object), then continue by stating a purpose why the spirit should choose to do so, and make it a good one. Deity will generally accept offers of worship in any form. Close and ground yourself.

You may need to sustain the spirit's interest, which can be done through often repeated rituals. These can be elaborate or simple. Burning incense once a day to a deity, for example, is sufficient as long as the mind is totally on the spirit form while performing the simple task.

To See Auras

Quite a lot has been written in the new age market about the ability to see auras. The human spirit, like all forms of Spirit, has sufficient substance that those with a certain degree of psychic sensitivity will naturally see the radius of energy which reaches beyond the physical body, and is detectable by Kirlian photography.

The method of seeing this extended spiritual substance is much like the methods for seeing nature spirits, and yet is easier for having the physical body as a central point of focus. If one looks at a person against a plain white background and either slightly unfocuses the eyes or simply stares long enough, the edges of the observed person will begin to glow, quite often in detectable colours. Seeing the extended aura to the point that Kirlian photography is able to reproduce is possible for some, especially with practice. In an ordinary situation where you may wish to observe a person's aura without the benefit of a selected plain background, it is often easiest to choose a section of their outline to focus on and follow the visual field around them from there. Again, this gets easier and easier with practice.

The mistake that some people make which creates a belief that they are unable to see auras is one of expectation. The colourful glow is not going to radiate in the same manner as a light bulb creating glowing effects. The aura is of Spirit, and vibrates at a very different frequency than ordinary light. Those who have trouble detecting the more subtle visual field may benefit from practising on themselves. One simple exercise for this is to stare at one's own hand for several minutes as it is held still over a plain background. Practising this daily for just a few days should bring some results even for the most resistant of subjects. Blind people will often be able to actually feel the substance of aura when passing their hands close to the skin of a person, and, like the sighted, can increase this ability with practice. Many meditation techniques increase awareness of one's own aura quite naturally, as a feeling of increased energy surrounding oneself which may be interpreted in a number of ways.

Another good exercise for learning to see one's own aura is to practice sitting in front of a full length mirror and staring into one's own eyes. This method can be used for a variety of meditation and self-discovery techniques as well, and may seem a bit difficult at first for those who have not practised meditation techniques before, but it is well worth persevering. In the act of focusing on the eyes, the peripheral vision becomes increasingly aware of the movement of subtle spiritual energies around oneself, and one of the biggest challenges of this method may be to remain focused rather than to look around to try to catch a better glimpse of what may be moving about so prolifically.

Healing Through Spirit

Becoming aware of one's own spiritual force, perhaps through observation of the aura, is a good first step toward spiritual healing. There are many methods that can be used for healing. They basically comprise either;

1) The transference of one's own spiritual force,
2) A form of sympathetic magic,
or
3) Calling on the forces of an outside spiritual entity.

Several of the world's religions allow for some form of direct spiritual healing. The beliefs behind the method and the level of dramatics can vary greatly, but at the root of the operation is a simple transference of one's own spiritual energies into another person who requires help. This can be a very draining task and may even lead to the healer becoming ill themselves if some provision is not made for replacing their own spiritual force. The wise healer will learn to draw energy from natural sources and effectively channel it through themselves and into the afflicted person. Practising aura magic can be very good for learning to manipulate energies in this way. One begins by practising the art of enlarging one's aura while meditating. After becoming proficient at this over time, the next step is to experiment with drawing energy from the spiritual forces of the elements available, most often Earth and Air. Experimentation is vital for mastering this technique. One must get the 'feel' of breathing energies in and out, drawing the elemental forces in and then cycling them back into the surroundings, and becoming part of the whole of the operation. Simply sucking energy from these sources is not as effective, it is more beneficial to keep all such spiritual essences in motion and flowing through oneself as a central point. Then the art of directing this force to where it is needed most naturally follows.

Sympathetic magic can take many forms as well. I gave the example in *Spirits of the Water* whereby a strip of cloth, originally an actual wound dressing, is left to moulder on the tree belonging to a sacred source of Water with the intent that the affliction will diminish with the cloth. Every culture has its own rituals for healing, which includes the Western cultural custom of swallowing tablets or pills. Some of these pills contain substances which act chemically to effect certain afflictions, but very often it is the actual act of swallowing the pill which is most effective. The belief of the afflicted person that the pill will effect a cure is a ritual of spirit which results in an internal transformation. Studies have been done with placebos to prove this many times over. This knowledge doesn't stop people like myself from reaching for the pills when minor illnesses arise, the cure is effected whether it is the substance of the pill at work or the belief which is actually effective. The principle is exactly the same as the methods of sympathetic magic which would be described as more 'primitive'. Shaking a rattle over an ill person to chase away evil spirits may well be just as effective for all of the same reasons.

Sympathetic magic consists of symbolising something which one wishes to happen or imitating the action one wishes to occur, followed by the result of the desired occurrence. A healing may be effected by drawing a sigil to become healthy, or any number of imitative actions such as when I knotted a rope to imitate the knitting of bone in a healing done on a horse's hoof which was briefly mentioned in the appendix of *Spirits of the Water*. After meeting and 'attuning' to the horse, I performed this sympathetic magic spell at home which basically consisted of finger knitting three strands of her tail with the rope and, with the help of my daughter who has had riding lessons and is very talented at this sort of magic anyway, performing an incantation while moving in a spiral spell pattern. The horse was completely healed, much to the confusion of the vet.

Any sort of imitative or symbolic action can be utilized in sympathetic magic, whether it is for healing or another purpose. In some healing cases, the healer can visualize and 'perform' actions such as dancing or some other happy activity with the afflicted person which the illness is preventing from actually happening, in order to create a link to the person with the image of wellness.

Another approach which uses visualization productively is to create an imaginary scenario where the healing agents of the body, the white blood cells, attack (in the form of jet fighters or other aggressive symbols) to attack an illness or bad cells. This has proven effective in some very serious illnesses.

The third method, calling upon an entity, is much like the first method only it involves absorbing Spirit and channelling it to the ill person. This is seen in faith healing and other religious performances. It can, however, be just as, if not more effective, with non-deified Aetherial spirits. Favourite Aetherial entities; fairies, Angels, deities and even daemonic or vampiric entities, can be called upon for healing purposes. The latter choices may not be preferred by sensible magicians unless they are well attuned to specific entities or have servitors used for the specific purpose of healing, but that does not negate the possibilities which exist for all denizens of the realm of Aether. Obviously an ill person is in no shape to begin a course of healing through demonology and would be better advised to seek familiar entities of an agreeable nature. Methods of using such things as vampiric energies for the relief of stress is a subject for another book and not recommended for random experimentation.

One of the oldest and most often used methods for spiritual self-healing is using simple meditation and visualization of white light. The principle behind this method is to seek balance throughout the spiritual body, which leads to similar balance within the physical body. Raising one's energy and creating a feeling of general well-being is one of the most effective methods for facilitating all other methods of healing, including using the benefits of medical science. The attitude of the patient is well known among doctors as an important ingredient in the overall prognosis of any affliction, serious or minor. This is why we have sayings like *"laughter is the best medicine."* As many magicians know, laughter is also an effective form of banishment.

Meditation: or Communing With One's Own Spirit

Meditation is frequently referred to in new age and magic books, yet seldom is any explanation given as to what the author means by this term apart from in books which are specifically written about the subject. There are exceptions where the author will describe the simple acts of sitting in a comfortable position, regular breathing and focusing the mind in some manner, but even when these basic instructions are given there seems to be an assumption that the reader will have some experience of these techniques and know exactly what the author means.

Chances are that anyone who picks up this book will have read others which will mention meditation, and may well have either read at least one book specifically about meditation or learned some techniques from someone, somewhere. However, I am going to give a little explanation here as to how meditation works with Spirit, as I feel it is appropriate to the references I have made in this section already.

Meditation happens in various forms. Those who study extreme disciplines of Eastern mysticism will encounter methods of mediation which involve sitting in very challenging positions rather than being told to sit comfortably as in many Western books about magic. There are good reasons for the positions in advanced meditation, and anyone who wishes to seriously study these disciplines is encouraged to seek appropriate instruction as this can benefit your spiritual advancement greatly.

The key word here however is 'discipline'. These are disciplines to be learned as a technique of their own rather than as a beginning step to ritual, as is the more relaxed version which is presented in most books on modern magic.

Meditation involves some level of a trance state, and that is the common ground between these two definitions of meditation. The contemplative state may be used for many purposes, and in some form is one of the most basic tenets of any spiritual path. Even the religions which claim to disagree with all things related to the 'new age' actually practice some form of meditation or contemplative state, although in extreme cases they may call it something else. In general, most Christian religions will encourage "prayer and meditation" to their devotees, meaning quiet contemplation rather than 'active meditation' as is practised in the aforementioned Eastern religions. Religions from other cultures may have a different word related to the native language of the culture which originates the religion, but the meaning will be the same.

Spirituality involves a certain amount of introspection. This is a part of meditation. For magical purposes, what is sought is the shift of mindset into a light trance state, or sometimes to a deeper state of alternate consciousness. The reason for this has much to do with focus, but it is also a method of accessing the subconscious mind which is where much of magic happens.

Most magical training programmes will begin with exercises in stillness under some name or other which is one form of meditation. One sits comfortably and clears the mind, thinking of nothing for several minutes or longer with practice. Easier said than done. Intruding thoughts are pushed aside as unimportant and the mind continues to wrestle with the normal busy thought processes, to quiet the incessant noise which traverses our normal waking consciousness far more than we would otherwise realize. This is an excellent exercise, and with practice can be very useful for many purposes. However, those who have trouble with this exercise should not give up and say that they are unable to meditate.

An alternate form of seeking clarity of the mind uses focus. Focus on breathing in to the count of four, stopping (without clenching the breath) for the count of four, and exhaling again to the count of four. This can include waiting for the count of four again before inhaling again, but works either way. Another method of focus mentioned in *Spirits of the Earth* is to strike a large stone with a dull knife repeatedly and slipping into trance as you focus on the rhythm. This can also be done with many other objects or instruments. Focusing on sound I find is a very effective method, and in fact the first time I ever reached a full meditative state was the result of sitting in front of a stereo speaker at a party when a particularly visual song was blasting, and in focusing and following the progression of the song I found myself transported first into intense visual images and then into my own head (no, there were no drugs involved). It was quite an amazing experience as I became aware of everything in the room despite having my eyes closed, as well as the visuals created by the music and a trance version of awareness which seemed to focus just above my own head as an astral entity.

Self-Transformation Spells

The essence of 'The Great Work' as it is referred to in Alchemical texts is in self-transformation, obstensibly to a 'higher spiritual state'. How such a 'higher state' is defined is another matter. The early Alchemists lived in a Christian world where much of what they believed was coloured by social acceptance and sometimes by the shadow of the inquisition. A basically Christian structure to their world view was a healthy thing at the time.

In today's world, spiritual progress may be measured in many ways and will vary in definition from one person to another. The original *Golden Dawn*'s emphasis on celibacy for spiritual 'purity' differs greatly from other group's attitudes of spiritual freedom through sexual freedom for example, yet both have validity for their adherents. Whether one approaches personal transformation through the disciplines of restriction, which can also apply to eating habits, forms of entertainment or many other things in modern society where choices are available to the average person, or through consciously liberating oneself from childhood programming and other limitations and taboos, the process of change is one of spiritual transformation which has long term effects on the overall character of the person who chooses a transformative path.

Not all personal transformation has to be an Earth shattering total diversity from a previous form of existence. Small self-transformations can be every bit as important to the individual and their personal spirituality. A decision to change one aspect of one's life, for example deciding to quit smoking, causes a larger degree of change in one's spiritual outlook than many people realize. This is even more significant if the process is approached through spiritual means rather than with an attitude of mundane deprivation for health or financial reasons.

In the magazine *Quest No. 119*, this is addressed in an article titled *Uncertainty, Chaos and the Atheist Pantheon* written by Frater M. Among other rather original ideas, Frater M explains a method of addressing such things as tobacco as Atheist demons which can be exorcised with similar methods as other demonic presences. He gives a five step programme which begins with identifying oneself not as a smoker trying to give up, but as a non-smoker who has been possessed by a smoking demon. Frater M has kindly given permission to quote the actual five steps from the article;

Step 1. Identify your smoking habit as an external demon. Recognise that you have been under possession from this demon and that it will attack you if you try to give up. Be confident that externalized, its power will be considerably weakened. The main way it tricked you before was by pretending that it was you and subverting your actions from within.

Step 2. Name the demon. Be creative. One way is to use an appropriate word and then reverse it to make it sound demonic. Fagash becomes *Fagashsagaf*, Smog becomes *Smogoms*, Dogend becomes *Dogendnegod* [this one is my favourite - JDH] etc.

Step 3. Create an image or effigy of the demon. Draw a picture of it or make a sculpture. If you're not a confident artist just draw a cigarette with an evil face on it. Write its name underneath. You could even draw the face on a real cigarette if you have one left!

Step 4. Prepare a ritual, include the image inside. Perform an evokation of the smoking demon. Calling it foul titles whilst saying its name three times out loud ought to be sufficiently dramatic to work. Banish it back to the foul and evil devil Tobacco. Burn or otherwise destroy the effigy as you do so [No, that doesn't mean you can smoke the cigarette with the face drawn on--JDH]. Before finishing the ritual in your usual manner, you could read out a liturgy of all the bad health effects of making a pact with the evil Tobacco devil, and all the environmental damage he causes. [Possibly followed by all the positive things which can be obtained through saved money?--JDH.]

Step 5. Being a smoker may have been a large or significant part of your persona. Having externalized and banished what you have now recognised as an external demon may leave you feeling a little empty or incomplete. This can be remedied by starting a new habit/behaviour pattern, this time a more healthy, environmentally friendly one. You can even finish the ritual in step four with a dedication to begin this new habit."

Having never been an actual smoker, I haven't had the opportunity to try this process as written, however, the concept is one of the most brilliant self-transformative ritual structures I have ever seen. The five steps could be applied to externalizing any personal habit or trait, or could be reversed to evoke a positive attribute one wishes to make a part of oneself and accepting it as a 'positive possession'.

Shifting Belief

Belief is a nebulous thing when it comes to the world of Spirit regardless of whether one is speculating on the origin and nature of the universe, or on much less momentous details of day to day existence. There are two most common beliefs about the origin of the universe, one by scientists (big bang) and one by the Christians and some other major religions (creation by a god), but what many people don't realise is that there are other theories as well. Chinese metaphysics purport the theory of natural causation much like Aristotle's theory of eternity and my own Time Continuum theory. The basis of all of these is that things exist in the universe. They always have, they always will. There is no beginning or end to time and matter. However, change is the natural order of the universe and can give the illusion of beginnings and endings. Things do not necessarily change for the better or for the worse, they simply change.

A person may have a hard and steadfast belief in a specific religious philosophy and for that person all aspects of the philosophy are true, yet another person with an entirely different religious philosophy (which may include science) with very different ideas may be as adamant that every aspect of their own belief is true, and therefore for them it is. Many people have more flexibility in their approach and may believe a basic philosophy or religion, but question various details about its interpretation. So what can be true? If a shift in belief can ascertain a shift in reality, then *nothing is true, and everything is permitted* [--Hassan i Sabbah]. One's perception at least of reality is greatly effected by chosen beliefs. It therefore follows that learning the art of shifting belief can lead to changes in perceived or even concrete reality, which is often referred to as *Magic*.

A shift in belief can allow one to accept that a computer generated spirit, chosen at random through the machinations of a mechanical device, can give concrete advice. The logical mind says that this is a game and not to be taken seriously, but one such device known as *Ghost in the Machine* has had some very spooky results for everyone I know who has tried it. The device can be found on the KIA website at http://wolf.chaosmagic.com

Learning the art of 'free belief' as described by Austin Osman Spare (Book of Pleasure) is probably one of the most valuable magical lessons that can be acquired. Early lessons in the power of divergent perception naturally open up the mind to boundless possibilities. Twenty-odd years ago, a five-year-old child in school was asked what the third day of the week is. He answered Wednesday. The teacher, however, said he was wrong and that it is Tuesday, because Sunday is the first day. That was when the child first realized that adults have differing perceptions, as his mother had taught him that it was Wednesday and he preferred her explanation to that of the teacher. He had instinctively discovered free belief, and grew up to be the most imaginative (and effective) magician I have ever met.

As I said in the section on meditation above, much of what makes magic happen occurs in the subconscious mind. The trick to performing magic in actual day to day practice and getting results lies largely in the ability to shift one's belief and *know* that whatever ritual process is involved, it will certainly work. This was recently demonstrated not once but twice to me by the above mentioned magician during holiday travel when trains were being cancelled and delayed on a regular basis. One of our trains was broken down at its point of origin, and at a spontaneous suggestion from me that he try a method recently read in Jan Fries' *Visual Magick*, he performed a simple ritual on the spot which resulted in a train appearing without explanation or announcement, which was going to our destination. The performance was repeated a couple of weeks later, when we had missed a connection due to a late first train and there just 'happened to be' another train with plenty of seats available ten minutes after we reached the connecting train station. The point is that we presumed there would be although we didn't know the time table.

Belief is the first step toward magical results. If I want it to rain, but look at the clear sky and say "not possible", then my belief that it cannot happen will prevent me from doing anything to effect a change. However, if I look at the clear sky and decide that a little condensation can escalate into the beginning of a cloud formation, which eventually can result in rain, it becomes possible. Possibility and 'chance' are effected by belief. This is a very basic tenet of magic.

As a magical exercise, it can be useful to believe something impossible every day. The sky is really pink, but light diffraction only makes it look that dull gray or blue; the person you went out with last night really will call today; the odd shape in the pattern on your wall is really the face of a benevolent damp spirit who will give good advice if you choose to listen; you will find a five pound note lying on the path through the park today when you walk through; you are actually a Pisces rather than a Gemini and will behave like one today. Any number of things can be imagined and practised as a belief, but what is the point of these bizarre imaginings? When you actually find the five pound note or the person calls, it will be obvious. Until then, imagining yourself as a different zodiac sign is a good exercise in the power of suggestion and the benevolent spirit just may tell you which path the note is waiting on...

Spawning An Aetherial Thought-Form

My advice for the beginning aspiring magician is: Don't. Try working with thought-forms from the basic elements as described in the previous volumes of this series first and get a feel for it. Those who jump right into conjuring thought-forms from Spirit will more often than not find themselves facing a hidden and possibly dark aspect of themselves which is borne of their own fears and misgivings about the unknown realms which they are just beginning to explore, and one shouldn't underestimate the power of one's own subconscious to SCARE ONE SILLY! Many good horror films have been produced to illustrate the point.

Having done my bit for dire warnings, let us continue for those with the experience or temerity to bypass such admonitions. I have said in the other volumes of this series that this is a matter for indoor working, except in the case of Fire thought-forms. Aetherial thought-forms may also be an exception. There is scope for both indoor and outdoor workings with these. Accessing Spirit may actually be done pretty much anywhere. However, everything I have said in the previous books about the chaotic or mischievous behaviour of thought-forms is particularly accentuated here.

Whatever old tomes of magic may say, an Aetherial spirit is never fully under the control of a magician, even when it is created by the magician from his or her own spirit as thought-forms are. Something which 'has spirit' is wild and free, apply this to your expectations of any spirit with which you deal magically. Having said that, one's expectations can make a big difference in the degree of direction which will be achieved. If you expect to be totally lacking in control in any magical operation, you get what you pay for. Expect absolute control but be ready to mop up when you lose it, and always keep a good banishing handy.

An Aetherial thought-form might be created for many possible purposes. They could potentially be used for any purpose in which another elemental spirit may be employed, but relegating creatures of Spirit to purposes with more specific associations is a bit like overkill. Think about your purpose carefully before making this choice. A purpose of Spirit may include things which affect your own spirit, philosophical questions, utopian ideals, healing a person with a psychiatric condition which is not otherwise defined as from physical causes, accessing Akashic records, finding one's way through a dilemma or many other purposes which could be defined as 'of Spirit'.

The method itself, although many variations exist, is much like that given in *Spirits of the Earth*. Create a central point which is where you intend to manifest the spirit. This may be a triangle within your ritual space in keeping with some old traditions, an object which is meant to represent the servitor you are creating for future use as well, or a container such as a little bottle to 'contain' a genius spirit. Open the ritual in your chosen manner and state your purpose in a specific and direct manner such as "*I wish to create a servitor for the purpose of* (state purpose)". As I have said many times before, be very specific about the purpose. You may wish to incorporate various methods into your ritual to 'charge' the servitor, such as sigil creation, dance magic, or any number of representative actions which apply to your intent.

At some point, circle the central point while performing some form of ritual whether it is in chant, dance, song, or drumming. Repeat your purpose many times within whatever medium you choose. Infuse the rite with your own spirit, allowing yourself to fully let go and 'become' the extant spirit as well as remaining yourself. A feeling of elation accompanies this form of self-release. Then realize yourself as separate from the created spirit and halt the proceedings, still infusing energy from yourself into the now separate part of yourself which has become the desired spirit. Release it by commanding it to go forth and accomplish its purpose, stating once again what that is as you do so. Close the ritual, ground and banish.

Grounding and Banishing

I have covered the subject of grounding and banishing fairly sufficiently in the previous volumes of this series, but in case of the unlikely event that the reader happens across this one first, I will repeat myself a bit here.

Grounding and banishing should generally be done after any ritual. There are a few exceptions, some of which have been specified throughout the series, but if there is any question it is best to err on the side of caution.

Grounding from the world of Spirit is much like any other grounding. After your final banishing or other finish of the ritual, send your energies into the Earth and eat something afterwards, preferably something sweet. Cakes and wine are brilliant for this, a feast is even better in a group situation where everybody brings something.

There are many methods of banishing residual energies. One very effective method which has become popular since the inception of the IOT is to banish by laughter. Everybody forces themselves to laugh, which soon becomes quite natural. It is surprisingly effective. More elaborate rituals can also be just as effective, it is a matter of what feels comfortable to the practitioner. Formally sending quarter guardians back to their realms is popular in Wiccan style rituals. Literally sweeping the ritual area while ritually dispelling residual spirits is also an old favourite.

Banishing Nefarious Entities

Many times I have come across people, particularly young people, who are in some way troubled by apparently nasty entities. They take many forms; a manic-depressive teenager believes he is disturbed at night by "Vampyre Shadows", another lad believes he is regularly "chased by demons" because someone else has told him that they put their "vampire mark" on him. A more mature friend of mine was startled one night when he saw a black shape at the end of his bed. Mistaking it for his flatmate, he pointed at it and said "You can't fool me, I'm on to you". The shape dissipated before my friend's eyes. There are many other examples, including the sort of entities which seem to be attracted by ouija boards, black dogs as described in an earlier chapter, etc.

What are these entities and how does one deal with them? Ninety-five percent of the time, they are created by their own victims. Not as figments of imagination, but as thought-form entities which the shaken victim is not aware of forming. These are projections, and like the dissipating entity above, can easily be dispelled by a confident confrontation.

But what of the other five percent, and how does one know the difference? The safe answer is to perform a proper banishing either way, as it will work as well on the thought-form as on a genuinely independent entity. However one's personal belief system may define these spirits, they can be attracted by interest in the occult as easily as conjured from stimulating the imagination and the thought-form variety can take on a presence very much like reality, so one of the first things for anyone interested in magic or spirits of any sort is to learn several banishings to deal with unwanted attention from such creatures.

The ritual closings in this series and other books on magic are good for dispelling much of unwanted energies. However, there are times when one may be attacked without having done any form of ritual, including the possibility of deliberate attacks from other magicians. I find that most people who believe that they are attacked by others are likely to be imagining such attacks through some form of internal guilt, but there are exceptions.

I once met someone who must have spent a fortune on mirrors because she imagined people magically attacking her all the time, but in reality nobody could be bothered. The woman was no real threat to anyone, apart from spreading ridiculous rumours about anyone she became jealous of (including me), and the magical community generally took little notice of her.

If the reader genuinely feels attacked by another person on a spirit level, a simple reversal spell which I will come to in a moment should suffice to eliminate the problem. For the moment, let's concentrate on demonic/vampiric entities of spirit.

In the earlier example when my friend was being followed by a black dog, his trained response was to draw a circle of protection in the ground in the manner of a particular magical system. He stayed in it all night. This is good if you are trained in a specific magical system, in which case you wont need me to tell you how to go about it. It is worth studying various magical systems in order to learn some of these techniques, but like martial arts, they must be properly learned until they are second nature. A few instructions in a book you read once aren't likely to be sufficient.

A good emergency banishing was created by Anton Channing, author of *Kaos Heiroglyphica*. It is called the *Starburst Banishing*, and was spontaneously created one night when he was a teenager, and was suddenly attacked by a demonic spirit of some sort. He had been visiting a friend's mother who had some 'new age' interests, and who had been sensing a presence outside the house. Anton, naturally sensitive to such presences, unintentionally drew its attention and it followed him when he left the house, walking home alone at night. The demon appeared in a parked car window, then suddenly it leaped onto him, engulfing him in darkness. This would be terrifying to even the most seasoned magician, yet he reacted instinctively with the following procedure;

The Starburst Banishing
(printed with permission)

1. Draw in a deep breath while curling up into a ball.

2. Visualize yourself becoming a black hole, sucking in everything around you.

3. When you are crammed to maximum capacity with energy you need to release it, like a quasar. A quasar has an accretion disc of orbiting matter that it is sucking into itself. However, the colossal energies involved mean that it has to release the energy it has absorbed in some way. It does this by firing out inner parts of the accretion disc as powerful beams of radiation and electrons. These fire outwards perpendicular to, and from the centre of, the disc.

4. Spin your quasar around in all directions so fast that you appear to be a massive ball emitting light in all directions. Anything that wasn't destroyed by being sucked into you will be hit by high energy radiation and evaporated. Breath out slowly as you do this.

5. Stand up straight and take a few deep breaths.

This method demonstrates one of the most basic principles of dealing with nefarious entities. Don't run. Turn on them and draw them into your own sphere of power. It takes a leap of faith the first time, but it's really quite easy to get the knack. These entities feed on fear and will certainly give chase if the intended victim runs. Like a wild animal, they interpret such action as identification of prey. And like *some* wild animals (don't test this on a grizzly bear!) will soon feel the tables turned if a confident person is drawing them in, taking control. Some forms of spirit can be contained, attached to an object, or even sent to be attached to other spirits, and this knowledge is a powerful weapon against demonic attack.

One method of getting rid of troublesome spirits is to create a talisman of some sort which will draw them into it if they get too close to you. I did this with a simple silver ring at the ripe old age of fifteen. It is a common age for attacks of this sort, and I had had a spate of 'sleeping attacks', where one reaches near wakefulness but is unable to finish waking as the presence of a nasty spirit becomes terrifying and seems to 'ride' the victim.

Creating such a talisman is a simple matter of choosing a piece of jewellery and performing a basic ritual on it; open, dedicate the item to absorbing nefarious or intruding entities while remembering the feel of that which has attacked you, close. Wear the item, always.

A Reversal Spell

Many books on magic provide reversal spells for those who feel they are under magical attack. These can be useful. However, the detrimental effect of having much literature available on psychic self-defense is that far too many people begin to feel that they are under attack too much of the time to have any basis in reality. Someone who imagines constant attack is likely to be primarily suffering the effects of their own ego, not realizing that very few magic users can be bothered to launch magical attacks at all, and even fewer have a clue as to how to go about it. Those who fall into the trap of performing never-ending mirror spells against imagined enemies eventually reach a stage where their own mirrors rebound their own negative energies back to them, thereby exacerbating the paranoia when things really do go wrong for them more than normally. It is simple bifurcation of their own paranoid energy, they are literally their own worst enemy.

A simple white candle spell I came up with about twenty-five years ago is still what I would recommend for suspected magical attack, as it allows for the possibility that the problem may be caused by another reason. In the instance when I first came up with it, it had been real. I knew this because what had been happening to me suddenly began to happen to someone else, she who had sent the spell. The reversal uses gentle enough energies that they will dissipate in time and leave the original victim truly free, because even revenge becomes a curse of sorts and ties one to the object of their vengeful feelings.

Having prattled on a bit now, the spell itself is almost embarrassingly simple. It is effectively a meditation, but one must be familiar with the 'feeling of ritual' to do it effectively. Open and close formally if you wish to, I don't bother for this one myself, although some preparation for the slip into 'ritual mode' is advised.

Light a single white candle in an appropriate holder. This is treated as a general spell, although the intent is specific. The candle should have been anointed with a favourite general oil. I use one called Druidic Holy Oil. Sit in front of the candle and focus, or rather unfocus, your vision just above the flame. Allow yourself to slip into trance, or 'ritual mode'. Then just state your purpose. I don't use rhyme for this one, just a simple statement such as "I feel magical interference, and send it back to its source." More specific explanation may be given according to circumstances, and an internal drama to relive the events which have led to the belief in magical attack accompanies the statement. Finish with a declaration of freedom from the interference, and a shielding. The shielding can take the form of a basic white light visualisation, which is generally effective even if it is a bit new age cliche'.

That's it, you're free. In Spirit, simple rituals are often the best and most easily effective. Much of the ritual forms one chooses should be a matter of whatever feels right for the practitioner. A magician with a physics degree may feel more comfortable with rituals that include complicated scientific paradigms, but most of us benefit just as much from very basic techniques.

And so we finish this series at last. I hope the reader will have benefited from the perceptions of Spirit which I have presented, but please always remember that Spirit is not static, but ever changing and approachable from many differing perceptions. Working magic in a world filled with spirits is an adventure with many chapters, and even my own perceptions as written have changed during the years I have spent writing about them for these books. That doesn't make the earlier volumes wrong, only slightly different than I might write them if I were to begin again from tomorrow. Spirit is not containable within the perceptive parameters that any one person may put on it. I would entreat the readers to examine closely their own perceptions and ideas of Spirit and to constantly re-examine those ideas as well as the thoughts of others, including myself, because no one philosophy contains all the secrets of what is a true definition of Spirit. Our own spirits evolve constantly as do our conceptions of Spirit. I leave this project with one last piece of spiritual advice: even reading a book on spiritual matters can cause one to slip into 'ritual mode', so ground yourself as you finish reading, perhaps with a nice bit of cake and a glass of wine, and leave behind for now, if you can, your time with the spirits of the Aether.

Bibliography

Alli, Antero. *Angel Tech: A Modern Shaman's Guide To Reality Selection*. Phoenix: Falcon Press, 1988.
Channing, Anton. *Kaos Heiroglyphica*. Norwich: KIA Press, 2001.
Coghlan, Ronan. *Handbook of Fairies*. Berkshire: Capall Bann Publishing, 1998.
Deary, Terry. *The Angry Aztecs*. London: Scholastic Ltd., 1997.
Dukes, Ramsay. *SSOTBME*. Surrey: Nigel Grey-Turner, 1979.
Fries, Jan. *Visual Magick*. Oxford: Mandrake of Oxford, 1992.
Grant, Kenneth. *Images and Oracles of Austin Osman Spare*. London: Frederick Muller Ltd., 1972.
Johnson, Caroline. *Angels*. London: Marshall Cavendish Limited, 1993.
Hawken, Paul. *The Magic of Findhorn*. London: Souvenier Press, 1975.
McLean, Adam. *A Treatise on Angel Magic*. Grand Rapids, MI: Phanes Press, 1990.
Mullin, Kay. *Wondrous Land-The Faery Faith of Ireland*. Berkshire: Capall Bann Publishing, 1997.
Roob, Alexander. *Alchemy & Mysticism*. Köln: Taschen, 1997.
Spence, Lewis. *British Fairy Origins*. Wellingborough: The Aquarian Press, Ltd., 1946.
Wildberg, Christian. *John Philoponus' Criticism of Aristotle's Theory of Aether*. Berlin: Walter De Gruyter, 1988.

Other Recommended Reading

De Valera, Sinead. *Fairy Tales of Ireland*. London: Four Square Books, 1967.
Evans-Wentz, W.Y. *The Fairy Faith in Celtic Countries*. New York: Citadel Press, 1990.
Hestleton, Phillip. *Secret Places of the Goddess*. Berkshire: Capall Bann Publishing, 1996.
MacLellan, Gordon. *Talking to the Earth*. Berkshire: Capall Bann Publishing, 1996.

Index

Aether, 2, 5-7, 9-13, 28, 30, 36, 49, 57, 61, 63, 67-68, 73, 87, 93, 99, 103-106, 108-111, 114-115, 121, 138-139
Aetherial, 6-8, 11, 13, 15, 19, 25, 41, 43-49, 51-52, 54, 57, 59-61, 63-65, 68-69, 72-73, 75-76, 83, 85-88, 90-91, 93, 95-96, 98, 101, 103-106, 108-109, 114-116, 120, 129-130
Air, 2, 5-6, 25, 44, 46, 59, 80, 106, 111-112, 114, 119
Akashic records, 8, 87, 131
alchemy, 80, 139
ancestor, 31, 37
angelic, 6, 15, 43-44, 49, 51, 54, 57, 59, 65, 70, 75-76
Angels, 8, 18-19, 22-23, 28, 46, 53, 63, 67, 77-80, 83, 106, 120, 139
Anton Channing, 81, 134
Aristotle, 5-7, 127, 139
Arthur Edward Waite, 77
Asana, 98
athame, 106-107
Austin Osman Spare, 15, 49, 53, 63, 85, 101, 128, 139
Azo, 87-88, 90

balance, 6, 9-11, 55, 61, 83, 90, 97, 114-115, 121
Bast, 97
black dog, 15, 51, 134
Book of Black Magic and of Pacts, 77

Caddy, Eileen, 59
Carroll, Peter J., 80, 98, 109
Chalice Well, 52
chaos, 5, 10, 12, 55, 67, 80, 90, 97, 107, 125
cut-ups, 94

daemon, 19, 114-115
De Philosophia, 6
Dee, Dr. John, 23, 76
deity, 52, 54, 67-68, 70, 72, 85, 87-88, 91, 96-98, 106-109, 111, 113-116
demonic, 6, 15, 19, 49, 53, 59-61, 65, 125, 134-135

Earth, 2, 5-6, 18, 25, 36-37, 41, 44, 46-47, 53, 55, 59, 67, 80-81, 85-87, 94-96, 103, 106, 111-112, 114, 116, 119, 123, 125, 131-132, 139
elemental, 1, 6, 11, 15, 25, 44, 46, 52, 57, 62, 73, 75, 83, 85, 94, 99, 105, 107, 119, 130
Enochian, 65, 70, 75-76

Faery, 19, 30, 46, 60-61, 65, 67, 70, 114, 139
fairies, 1-2, 8, 11, 13, 17-19, 28, 46, 49, 53-54, 61, 68, 71, 95, 106, 120, 139
Fairy Hill, 16-17, 53
fairy mist, 8, 46, 60
familiar, 44, 72-73, 83, 93, 96, 121, 137

Fantasia, 86
fasting, 71
Findhorn, 59, 114, 139
First Matter, 5, 80
Frater M, 0, 81, 125
Free Belief, 85, 128
Fries, Jan, 128

ghosts, 13, 18, 24, 28, 41, 44, 53
Glastonbury Tor, 52
gnosis, 63, 82
god form, 44, 95, 97
goddesses, 8, 28, 81, 97, 106
gods, 8, 25, 28, 36, 44, 97, 106, 115
Golden Dawn, 65, 124
Gottfried Leibniz, 80
'The Great Work', 124
Guardian Angels, 22
guardian, 8, 22-23, 86-87, 90, 95, 114

Hathor, 97
Hawken, Paul, 59
healing, 87, 118-121, 131
Horus, 97
House Spirits, 22-23, 68

Images and Oracles of Austin Osman Spare, 53, 139
incubus, 19
invite, 54, 112, 114-115
Isle of Man, 16, 21, 53

Jack-in-a-box, 19
Kenneth Grant, 53
Key of Solomon the King, 76
Kirlian photography, 117
Kobold, 19

Laveaux, Marie, 40-41
Lavosier, 7

lemniscate, 6
Liber Null, 98, 109
The Lion King, 31
Lourdes, 44, 52

MacGregor Mathers, George, 76
magic squares, 75-76
Mauthe Doo, 20-22
meditation, 52, 59, 77, 93-94, 96, 98, 117-118, 121-123, 128, 137
monads, 80
Morrison, Jim, 38, 52
Mulan, 31

Necronomicon, 54, 65
Nirvana, 37

Ordo Templi Orientis, 65
ouija, 93, 95, 133

peyote, 93
poltergeist, 23-25, 53-54
Pranayama, 98
prayer, 59, 65, 93, 95, 105-106, 110, 122
primordial chaos, 5, 12
protection, 51, 70, 87, 113, 134
purification, 90, 106

Queen Maeve, 19

religion, 7, 13, 31, 72, 123, 127

Santeria, 93
Sekhmet, 97
self-transformation, 8, 61, 67, 104, 124
servitor, 21, 85-87, 90-91, 96, 131
shadow, 10, 18, 124
Sidhe, 70
sigil, 72, 76-77, 120, 131

141

Sin Eater, 71
spirit guides, 15
Spirit, 2, 5-13, 15, 18-19, 21-25, 28, 36-37, 41, 43-49, 51-54, 56-57, 59-65, 67-73, 75-76, 82-83, 86-89, 93-96, 98-101, 103-106, 108-122, 127, 129-132, 134-138
Spirits of the Air, 46
Spirits of the Earth, 46-47, 53, 55, 67, 80, 85-86, 95, 103, 114, 116, 123, 131
Spirits of the Water, 60, 75, 85, 119-120
succubus, 19
superstition, 11, 40-41
symbols, 6-8, 67, 73, 75, 120

Temple, 8, 24, 44, 47, 54, 60, 67, 69-70, 86, 89-90, 105, 114-115
The Magic of Findhorn, 59, 139
The Starburst Banishing, 134-135
theology, 7
thought-form, 13, 19, 21, 23-25, 46, 54, 69, 82-83, 85-90, 129-130, 133
time continuum, 6, 127
trance, 77, 94, 122-124, 137
Tuatha de Danaan, 19, 53
Uncertainty, Chaos and the vacuity, 63
vampire, 54, 106, 133
vampiric spirits, 8
vampyre, 19, 28, 61, 65, 132
Van Gelder, Dora , 67
visual perception, 2, 49
Voudon, 93

wand, 106-107
Watchers, 22, 44
Wona of the Mist, 18

yoga, 93, 98

FREE DETAILED CATALOGUE

Capall Bann is owned and run by people actively involved in many of the areas in which we publish. A detailed illustrated catalogue is available on request, SAE or International Postal Coupon appreciated. **Titles can be ordered direct from Capall Bann, post free in the UK** (cheque or PO with order) or from good bookshops and specialist outlets.

Do contact us for details on the latest releases at: **Capall Bann Publishing, Auton Farm, Milverton, Somerset, TA4 1NE.** Titles include:

A Breath Behind Time, Terri Hector
Angels and Goddesses - Celtic Christianity & Paganism, M. Howard
Arthur - The Legend Unveiled, C Johnson & E Lung
Astrology The Inner Eye - A Guide in Everyday Language, E Smith
Auguries and Omens - The Magical Lore of Birds, Yvonne Aburrow
Asyniur - Womens Mysteries in the Northern Tradition, S McGrath
Beginnings - Geomancy, Builder's Rites & Electional Astrology in the European Tradition, Nigel Pennick
Between Earth and Sky, Julia Day
Book of the Veil, Peter Paddon
Caer Sidhe - Celtic Astrology and Astronomy, Vol 1, Michael Bayley
Caer Sidhe - Celtic Astrology and Astronomy, Vol 2 M Bayley
Call of the Horned Piper, Nigel Jackson
Cat's Company, Ann Walker
Celtic Faery Shamanism, Catrin James
Celtic Faery Shamanism - The Wisdom of the Otherworld, Catrin James
Celtic Lore & Druidic Ritual, Rhiannon Ryall
Celtic Sacrifice - Pre Christian Ritual & Religion, Marion Pearce
Celtic Saints and the Glastonbury Zodiac, Mary Caine
Circle and the Square, Jack Gale
Compleat Vampyre - The Vampyre Shaman, Nigel Jackson
Creating Form From the Mist - The Wisdom of Women in Celtic Myth and Culture, Lynne Sinclair-Wood
Crystal Clear - A Guide to Quartz Crystal, Jennifer Dent
Crystal Doorways, Simon & Sue Lilly
Crossing the Borderlines - Guising, Masking & Ritual Animal Disguise in the European Tradition, Nigel Pennick
Dragons of the West, Nigel Pennick
Earth Dance - A Year of Pagan Rituals, Jan Brodie
Earth Harmony - Places of Power, Holiness & Healing, Nigel Pennick
Earth Magic, Margaret McArthur

Eildon Tree (The) Romany Language & Lore, Michael Hoadley
Enchanted Forest - The Magical Lore of Trees, Yvonne Aburrow
Eternal Priestess, Sage Weston
Eternally Yours Faithfully, Roy Radford & Evelyn Gregory
Everything You Always Wanted To Know About Your Body, But So Far Nobody's Been Able To Tell You, Chris Thomas & D Baker
Face of the Deep - Healing Body & Soul, Penny Allen
Fairies in the Irish Tradition, Molly Gowen
Familiars - Animal Powers of Britain, Anna Franklin
Fool's First Steps, (The) Chris Thomas
Forest Paths - Tree Divination, Brian Harrison, Ill. S. Rouse
From Past to Future Life, Dr Roger Webber
Gardening For Wildlife Ron Wilson
God Year, The, Nigel Pennick & Helen Field
Goddess on the Cross, Dr George Young
Goddess Year, The, Nigel Pennick & Helen Field
Goddesses, Guardians & Groves, Jack Gale
Handbook For Pagan Healers, Liz Joan
Handbook of Fairies, Ronan Coghlan
Healing Book, The, Chris Thomas and Diane Baker
Healing Homes, Jennifer Dent
Healing Journeys, Paul Williamson
Healing Stones, Sue Philips
Herb Craft - Shamanic & Ritual Use of Herbs, Lavender & Franklin
Hidden Heritage - Exploring Ancient Essex, Terry Johnson
Hub of the Wheel, Skytoucher
In Search of Herne the Hunter, Eric Fitch
Inner Celtia, Alan Richardson & David Annwn
Inner Mysteries of the Goths, Nigel Pennick
Inner Space Workbook - Develop Thru Tarot, C Summers & J Vayne
Intuitive Journey, Ann Walker Isis - African Queen, Akkadia Ford
Journey Home, The, Chris Thomas
Kecks, Keddles & Kesh - Celtic Lang & The Cog Almanac, Bayley
Language of the Psycards, Berenice
Legend of Robin Hood, The, Richard Rutherford-Moore
Lid Off the Cauldron, Patricia Crowther
Light From the Shadows - Modern Traditional Witchcraft, Gwyn
Living Tarot, Ann Walker
Lore of the Sacred Horse, Marion Davies
Lost Lands & Sunken Cities (2nd ed.), Nigel Pennick
Magic of Herbs - A Complete Home Herbal, Rhiannon Ryall
Magical Guardians - Exploring the Spirit and Nature of Trees, Philip Heselton
Magical History of the Horse, Janet Farrar & Virginia Russell
Magical Lore of Animals, Yvonne Aburrow
Magical Lore of Cats, Marion Davies
Magical Lore of Herbs, Marion Davies

Magick Without Peers, Ariadne Rainbird & David Rankine
Masks of Misrule - Horned God & His Cult in Europe, Nigel Jackson
Medicine For The Coming Age, Lisa Sand MD
Medium Rare - Reminiscences of a Clairvoyant, Muriel Renard
Menopausal Woman on the Run, Jaki da Costa
Mind Massage - 60 Creative Visualisations, Marlene Maundrill
Mirrors of Magic - Evoking the Spirit of the Dewponds, P Heselton
Moon Mysteries, Jan Brodie
Mysteries of the Runes, Michael Howard
Mystic Life of Animals, Ann Walker
New Celtic Oracle The, Nigel Pennick & Nigel Jackson
Oracle of Geomancy, Nigel Pennick
Pagan Feasts - Seasonal Food for the 8 Festivals, Franklin & Phillips
Patchwork of Magic - Living in a Pagan World, Julia Day
Pathworking - A Practical Book of Guided Meditations, Pete Jennings
Personal Power, Anna Franklin
Pickingill Papers - The Origins of Gardnerian Wicca, Bill Liddell
Pillars of Tubal Cain, Nigel Jackson
Places of Pilgrimage and Healing, Adrian Cooper
Practical Divining, Richard Foord
Practical Meditation, Steve Hounsome
Practical Spirituality, Steve Hounsome
Psychic Self Defence - Real Solutions, Jan Brodie
Real Fairies, David Tame
Reality - How It Works & Why It Mostly Doesn't, Rik Dent
Romany Tapestry, Michael Houghton
Runic Astrology, Nigel Pennick
Sacred Animals, Gordon MacLellan
Sacred Celtic Animals, Marion Davies, Ill. Simon Rouse
Sacred Dorset - On the Path of the Dragon, Peter Knight
Sacred Grove - The Mysteries of the Forest, Yvonne Aburrow
Sacred Geometry, Nigel Pennick
Sacred Nature, Ancient Wisdom & Modern Meanings, A Cooper
Sacred Ring - Pagan Origins of British Folk Festivals, M. Howard
Season of Sorcery - On Becoming a Wisewoman, Poppy Palin
Seasonal Magic - Diary of a Village Witch, Paddy Slade
Secret Places of the Goddess, Philip Heselton
Secret Signs & Sigils, Nigel Pennick
Self Enlightenment, Mayan O'Brien
Spirits of the Air, Jaq D Hawkins
Spirits of the Earth, Jaq D Hawkins
Spirits of the Earth, Jaq D Hawkins
Stony Gaze, Investigating Celtic Heads John Billingsley
Stumbling Through the Undergrowth , Mark Kirwan-Heyhoe
Subterranean Kingdom, The, revised 2nd ed, Nigel Pennick
Symbols of Ancient Gods, Rhiannon Ryall

Talking to the Earth, Gordon MacLellan
Taming the Wolf - Full Moon Meditations, Steve Hounsome
Teachings of the Wisewomen, Rhiannon Ryall
The Other Kingdoms Speak, Helena Hawley
Tree: Essence of Healing, Simon & Sue Lilly
Tree: Essence, Spirit & Teacher, Simon & Sue Lilly
Through the Veil, Peter Paddon
Torch and the Spear, Patrick Regan
Understanding Chaos Magic, Jaq D Hawkins
Vortex - The End of History, Mary Russell
Warp and Weft - In Search of the I-Ching, William de Fancourt
Warriors at the Edge of Time, Jan Fry
Water Witches, Tony Steele
Way of the Magus, Michael Howard
Weaving a Web of Magic, Rhiannon Ryall
West Country Wicca, Rhiannon Ryall
Wildwitch - The Craft of the Natural Psychic, Poppy Palin
Wildwood King , Philip Kane
Witches of Oz, Matthew & Julia Philips
Wondrous Land - The Faery Faith of Ireland by Dr Kay Mullin
Working With the Merlin, Geoff Hughes
Your Talking Pet, Ann Walker

FREE detailed catalogue and FREE 'Inspiration' magazine
Contact: Capall Bann Publishing, Auton Farm, Milverton, Somerset TA4 1NE

Capall Bann has moved from Berkshire and is now at:

*Auton Farm
Milverton
Somerset
TA4 1NE*

*Tel 01823 401528
www.capallbann.co.uk
enquiries@capallbann.co.uk*

A full detailed catalogue is available on request

Capall Bann has moved from Berkshire and is now at:

Auton Farm
Milverton
Somerset
TA4 1NE

Tel 01823 401528
www.capallbann.co.uk
enquiries@capallbann.co.uk

A full detailed catalogue is available on request